A realm of pure bliss

Description of four days in the land of Vraja

Table of Contents

PREFACE

Sorrow has always dominated the world. Even with momentary occasions of happiness, the shadow of distress forever follows. From time immemorial, there have been lots of motivations and inspirations that are aimed to lighten the burden of worry and distress from the minds of humans. But time is witness that it is only the glories of Sri Hari that have managed to give solace to the hearts of yearning souls in reality.

With so much of mind blogging content available through multiple channels, this piece of work aims to bring some happiness to people. Without including any thrill, philosophy, analysis or lowering dignity of any characters involved, this book will simply cause happiness to those who read it.

This work was prompted for the younger generations who keep interests in keeping in touch with various types of media and hanker with so many bondages in the mind. Such material should prove to relax them to some extent.

It is evident that in today's date, content that accelerates adrenaline production is very much sought after but again it is further evident that the minimal delight that it provides usually ends up shading the minds and hearts of the audience with so much of darkness. Just as genes are transferred from a myriad previous generations without knowledge, each and everything that our senses (including the mind) relate to are kept within the intellect until times beyond our thoughts. If we keep feeding ourselves with negative, vulgar, harsh, scary and disturbing content, it is but obvious that the vibrations we will emanate are going to act negatively; on ourselves and others surrounding us.

With these aspects in mind, I bring out to you a vivid description of a few days in the supreme abode of vraja in the association of Lord Krishna and his acquaintances. With simplicity in subject and sweetness in content, this is a presentation of ultimate positivity for whoever who reads it. Irrespective of your personal concepts, this work is intended to bring out true smiles on your face; not just superficially but right from your soul!

I would like to dedicate this book to my parents Dr. N. Chaturvedi and Dr. P. Chaturvedi who sowed in the seed of bhakti in me at the right age – from birth, and to my sister Dr. M. Tripathi who helped me grow that seed into a sapling and then a plant.

My sincere gratitude goes out to the artists involved in this work. All art work that has been included in this book has been laid out with pure love and devotion as a service to the Lord. I got associated with some amazing artists who were of such high caliber yet so humble. I cannot thank each of them enough for their valuable assistance in this work. The artists for this work are Dr. Mukta Tripathi, Tista Tiwari, Krishna Suresh, Priyanka Gupta, Shuchi Mishra, Parimala Bhakta Sohoni and Chhaya Garhewal. My special thanks to Keshav anna and Govind anna who own the brand "Krishna for today" and readily agreed to provide me soft copies of some of their most expensive works for perusal in my book. Solely being artists, their contribution deserves specific highlight and I am very grateful for their loving assistance. I would also like to thank the brother sister duo Ankur

Agarwal and Priyanshi Agarwal for lending me some of the fantastic photographs that they have captured with so much love in the present day land of Vraja Bhumi. We can still experience the same divinity of yester times if we visit Vraja with a cleansed heart. These photographs stood proof for the same.

A huge lot of work was done in the launch of this book and the appreciation and motivation received by some of my contributors was exceptional. A special mention is necessary to Tista Tiwari, Vishali Naren and Krishnaswamy Ramarathnam uncle for giving their blessings in the form of a video for the pre launch of this book. I would also like to specifically thank Vishali Naren, a dear friend of mine, for giving such a strong foreword for this book and my mother for decorating my work with her blessings in words!

Last but not the least, I would like to gratefully thank my husband, Kanhaiya Upadhyay, and my son, Sudarshan for not only being patient with my involvement in this work but also for being extremely motivating and encouraging at every step of my life. If it was not for them, none of my works would be possible.

"sarvam sri krishnarpanamastu"
Offering this book to the lotus feet of Sri Krishna

FOREWORD

~Vishali Naren
(Entrepreneur, Book Enthusiast, Advocate of Disability Rights, Motivational Blogger, Translator)

Our scriptures have long acted as motivational and inspirational works apart from being the source of life. Almost all positive quotes and sayings find root in our scriptures. It is not surprising that our previous generations based their lives on them and it is rather sad that the current generation has drifted away from them. Considering these situations, it is important now than never before, that the knowledge and content of our shastras are brought forward in an easy format for today's legion to grasp.

Just like her previous works, Ojaswita has once again presented a work of great depth tailored with simplicity. A realm of pure bliss is a book of therapeutic nature, solely designed to generate positivity, especially among the young generation.

With Krishna as the subject, the book revolves around kathas from the Bhagavata Purana and other similar sources. It is authentic and at the same time presented in a manner which appeals to the current era. The book acts as a bridge for each reader to connect with oneself, nature and other people as well. I consider it as an indispensable instrument to restore balance of thought in the human mind, considering the amount of negativity we're surrounded by in the present times.

Wishing her all the best, I sincerely hope that Ojaswita's work reaches out to the world spurring the positivity driven by intention, conceptualization and action in the form of "A Realm of Pure Bliss"!!

BLESSINGS

~Prof. (Mrs). Padmaja Chaturvedi (Retd)
(Mother)

The book is a sweet presentation of sweetest past times of Bal Gopal. The author finds the real bliss in describing the first four days of herding only calves by Bal Krishna along with his friends in Vrindavan around Goverdhan hills. The description includes the performance of rituals by Brahmins to begin the herding of calves by five years old Nand Nandan on Gopastami, special preparation s and emotions of mother Yashoda and Nand Baba, enthusiasm of Balram and his friends at their levels and past times of Bal Gopal in Vrindavan while calves were busy grazing.

The book reflects the real picture of Leela described in Bhagvaan in English so that our young generation who do not have knowledge of Sanskrit can also enjoy and experience the bliss of Krishna Leela.

(Artist: Krishna Suresh)

naveena megha sannibham
suneela shyamalachchavi
suhaas ranjitaadharam
namami Krishna sundaram

"I bow down to that Krishna, who has the hue of a fresh rain cloud and whose bluish form represents youthfulness, whose lips are decorated with a beautiful smile and who is the very epitome of beauty!"

DAY 1 – *THE FIRST DAY OF HERDING*
The Preparation

"Has he not woken up Aunt Yashoda?" exclaimed a surprised Subala.

"Oh! He promised to be up very soon as it is our first day to herd the calves in the forest. The Brahmins have deduced the best day to start today – the eighth day of the bright fortnight in the propitious month of Kartik. We'd better wake him soon before the auspicious time passes!" added on Madhumangala.

"He was excited out of bounds last night and so kept on peeping out of the windows till late. Come on in fast, let's get him out of bed!" said Balarama as he swiftly came out of the bejeweled corridors of the palace of Nanda Maharaj. The boys were contented to see him – his bright aura and blue garments. Whirling around his herding stick in enthusiasm, he appeared to be veera rasa personified; augmented with beauty and dignity. Yashoda embraced him. She could feel her heart sooth as he loved her back.

"You are right my son! I'm sure Kanha must have been awake till late due to excitement. Let's go boys. Come help me wake your friend." Yashoda moved like a queen towards the bed chamber of Krishna. On her way, her servants accompanied her seamlessly. It was almost a daily routine for everyone in Vraja – as Surya narayan arose from the eastern horizon, everyone would finish their daily chores and worship and head off towards Nand Mahal to catch a glimpse of their beloved Gopala. And the same happened today as well. Gradually, everyone arrived. It was a ceremony each day to wake this little darling.

"Wake up! O dear son of the king of vraja! The lotus flowers have blossomed by the touch of sunrays. The water lilly flowers have shrunk back as the moon has departed and swarms of bees are wandering on the hanging creepers. Listen to the sound of the birds in the forest and the cows in their cowshed that are running towards their calves. The moon has lost its luster and the sun shines bright as men and women sing alike. O beloved Shyam of Soordas who carries a lotus in his hands! The dawn has set, do wake up!"

It was not long before Krishna opened his beautiful eyes with kohl spread out due to rubbing. His heart – stealing glances simply delighted everyone. He jumped out of bed exclaiming "Mother! I hope I'm not late! It's my first day of herding; I must complete my chores fast!"

The entire room was filled with vibrancy. As long as Gopala was asleep, vraja mandala would also be subtle. It was his awakening that actually started the day. Yashoda grabbed her son towards her heart – she had missed him through the night. She smiled and assured him that there was ample time yet. The sun had just risen. Daily chores were fulfilled.

(Artist: Dr. Mukta Tripathi)

And today another bright day had begun. It was a special day today. The troupe of boys was thrilled that they were officially being allowed to herd the calves. Nand maharaj entered the palace with a group of Brahmins. Special ceremonies had to be fulfilled today as the boys were to begin something very important. Krishna and Balarama saw him from afar. It was one of the rare days that he was not there when his dear son had woken up. The boys rushed to him and entered his cuddle. He took them to the arena where all ceremonial amenities were kept. The prayers were performed successfully and the boys were ready to move on.

Yashoda's heart skipped a beat. Her son was going to be away from her, even if it was for a little while. She had everything in her mind – pride, worry, happiness, anxiety, joy and every mixture of emotions. But her inner self knew that her boy was never going to be away from her in reality. She stepped towards the kitchen to pack up the lunch for the boys. It was a feast everyday in the kitchen of mother Yashoda. All six types of tastes including salty, sweet, sour, bitter, pungent and astringent, were always present in her kitchen, which was immensely blessed by Annapoorna. She thought of packing but stopped for a while. She was worried and sent out a servant to call Balarama. When it came to the protection of Krishna, Yashoda was confident only on Balarama.

Balarama was the epitome of enthusiasm. As he entered the kitchen, he went up to mother Yashoda.

"Do you need help mother? Can I assist you with packing our lunches?"

"Not at all darling! I want to tell you something very important. Krishna is mischievous by nature and never gives up any opportunity of adventure. This is the first time he will be going away without adult supervision. I cannot trust his pranks and I fear that he should not get into any type of trouble. I am entrusting his protection to you, I am confident that nothing can go wrong if you are with him. Please take care of Krishna!"

"You need not say it mother! He will be under my care and control. Please rest assured."

His sweet and convincing words could not be overlooked and were enough for Yashoda. She quickly ran her hands through the myriad dishes that she had prepared with much love for all the boys. She was a master at everything she laid her hands on. From the taste of the food to the packing, perfection was compromised nowhere.

Heading out

The boys were already in the cowshed caressing the calves. The numbers had almost doubled in the cowshed of Nanda maharaj since all the boys had brought their calves as well. But surprisingly, since the birth of their princes – Krishna and Balarama, there had been no lessening in vraja. Even mother earth seemed to expand her vicinities beyond boundaries to engulf all the love that was overflowing. And that is why even if numbers doubled, space was still plentiful. That is the glory of true love. True love can expand beyond boundaries and nurture to the fullest, it can help you arise beyond limitations and give abundantly, it never ruins you; it gives you immensely in return. Such love is transcendental, possibly only found in the realm of Krishna.

The servants of Nand mahal came with the lunch packs and handed over to the boys. Tosha took over the food management. "Goodies need to be kept away from Madhumangala lest we find them all finished! If there is one thing we cannot entrust him with, it is our foodstuffs!" he jokingly said and all other friends laughed in agreement. The calves were excited too. Harini and Hamsini (Krishna's favorite calves) would not leave Krishna's side. They would be with him for such a long time and were already imagining of the fresh green grass together with his flute. Their mothers did not want them to part but surely wanted them to enjoy the association of Krishna.

With sweet sounds of swastivachana from the Brahmins, the first herding journey began. Mother Yashoda came once again to instruct the boys.

"Keep in mind not to wander away too deep in the forest. Keep calm near the waters of Yamuna and do not climb too high on Govardhana! Keep your eyes on the calves and do a good job. And all of you remember that any pranks will not be out of my knowledge!"

All the other ladies of vraja and mothers of the cowherd boys supported with their instructions too. The boys nodded in commitment and promised to abide by their orders. They felt grown up and very proud of themselves. At that moment, mother Yashoda noticed that none of the boys had their footwear on.

"Why haven't you all put your footwear?"

Gasping at each other, the gopas just kept quiet. After all, they had one simple reason for almost everything they did – "because Krishna said". Gopala stepped forward.

"Mother, how can I wear footwear when all my calves will go barefoot?"

Krishna's love was naturally astounding for everything and everyone. It was much more for those who loved him back; they obviously got reciprocation beyond their expectations. Although his answer regarding footwear did not seem realistic in any sense, the affection was too large to be checked by practicality. Elders present at the scene purely smiled in fondness and made way for the team to move ahead.

Krishna played his sweet flute and the calves ran ahead in herds. Krishna and Balarama together with their friends followed them next. They swiftly moved through the lanes of habitats of Nandagao and headed towards vrindavana.

The elegance of Vrindavana

Vrindavana – the divine territory of splendor became even more divine as Krishna had blessed her with his presence. The trees were beautifully decorated by green creepers that surrounded them, overloaded with brightly coloured flowers which they showered upon the battalion of gopas as they passed underneath. Birds on the trees chirped in happiness as they saw Shyama and Balarama come along towards their home, peacocks danced in fervor and parrots flew above making the blue sky look adorned with green ink. The sun wanted to come closer and view this extraordinary scene of the supreme brahma enjoying amidst cows and cowherds, but he feared that his heat would be uncomfortable for the tender little boys, and so he hid behind the large clouds and caught heartwarming glimpses. Flowers blossomed with happiness and bees sung merrily as they swayed together. It was bliss to be there. Staring from above, the demigods wished that they could have a fraction of that bliss. Their paradise was rather bland in front of the abundant pleasure of love that they viewed in Vrindavana. Pondering over how futile their pleasures were, the demigods questioned their destiny.

Vrindavana kyu na bhaye hum mor
Karat nivas govardhana upar nirakhat nand kishor
Kyu na bhaye bansi kula sajani adhar peevat ghana ghor
Kyu na bhaye gunja ban beli rahat shyam ju ki or
Kyu na bhaye makarakrita kundala shyam shravana jhak jhor
Paramanand das ko thakur gopin ke chita-chor

"Why did I not become a peacock in the land of Vrindavana. I would reside on the Govardhana hill and continuously gaze at the son of Nanda! Why was I not born as one of the bamboo sticks (so that I may have been used to make his flute) and got the opportunity to relish the ambrosia of his lips! Or even just a creeper of the gunja flower in the forest whom he would cling on to! Why could I have not been the shark shaped earrings that move valiantly in his ears! The Lord of Paramanand das is he who has stolen the hearts of the gopis!"

Such was the glorious land of Vrindavana; gracefully tinged with the love of Krishna in every atom thus radiating an aura of pure bliss. Real bliss is that which transverses beyond the materialistic nature and touches the soul. That bliss is so rare that even the demigods declared that their heavenly pleasures were not even equal to the flora and fauna of vrindavana.

Vrindavana was the reflection of the love that overflowed in Krishna's heart. Its lands welcomed the calves and cowherd boys with utmost warmth and they all diverged out on the lush greenery. The calves swerved like water flowing from a river and began relishing the grass while enjoying the open environment of the forest. The young lads settled under a large banyan tree. Some climbed up the tree and rested themselves there. Others surrounded Krishna and Balarama by roots and relaxed as the cool breeze blew across bringing with it the fragrance of fresh flowers. They made fans from lotus leaves from the backwaters of the river Yamuna and helped themselves with more air.

Time and again, a small group of boys went to tend the calves and make sure that they did not wander far away in the forest.

As the sun rose higher, the calves wished to have some water. Shridama was the first to sense this. He was acquainted with a special capability to sense even the smallest difficulty that any living being had. It was possibly the aura that he was brought up in. Barsana was known to be house to compassionate souls and he was the prince of Barsana, the son of King Vrishabhanu and the brother of Radha who was known for her concerned nature.

"Shouldn't we move towards a water reservoir Krishna? The calves have been feeding for quite some time and should need water now. Plus, we also want to spend time on the supple soft sand banks of mother Yamuna. Isn't it friends?" said Shridama

Madhumangala and Subala were excited, they would never miss any chance to swim. But Madhumangala was more interested because he knew that once they reach the river, lunch will be unpacked soon. And all the boys agreed at once to Shridama's words. Krishna stood up and stretched his arms. The petite child appeared as if Lord Vamana was in the process of enlarging his body. As he slowly squeezed back and pulled his flute out, it was evident that he was on an endeavor of victory just like Lord Vamana, but this time through musical love. Troupes of calves and cowherds followed him like a bunch of maddened bees towards a swaying flower.

Krishna led his group towards Kamyavan – the enchanting, ever attractive forest. This area was beautified by nature in her blushing youth. And when nature bestows her beauty, nothing can beat the splendor. Predominance of small plants in this forest allowed for everyone to view its brilliance afar. The soft breezes cooled the boys and calves as they entered kamyavan. Slowly, they all moved towards the pond and halted. Sweet smelling fragrances of freshly bloomed lotuses enthralled the senses and numerous plantations around the area appeared to be welcoming the boys by spreading their leaves on the ground for seats. Krishna and Balarama rested in the companionship of the shrubs. Madhumangala, Tosha and Shridama directly jumped into the pond with other boys for a well awaited swim. Subala's nature was rather calm; he decided to rest for a while before indulging into the waters. Being a cousin to Krishna and Balarama, he was dearly loved by both of them and they offered him a seat in between themselves. They all spread their legs outwards and stretched their bodies. Exchanging brief topics about the family, cows and other cousins, they spent some quality time among themselves.

"Come on Krishna! The waters are so cool, how are you three able to resist a swim. Come in, please. Let's have some good time together in this awesome pond!" said Shridama after a few minutes.

"Let's go Krishna, come Subala." Said Balarama as he got up and lend his hand for the other two boys. His energy and strength were unmatchable; both Krishna and Subala held his left hand together and got up.

All the boys enjoyed water sports for some time.

"Tosh! You mentioned that there was a special step that you would teach us which could be done under water. Why don't you take a go now!" shouted Madhumangala from the other side of the pond as he came swimming.

Tosha was the dance expert in the group of friends. His ability of performing this art was incomparable; the elders hailed him as the gandharva of vraja. All performances for every ceremony in vraja were conducted under his guidance. Quite naturally, his friends would also brush off some talent from him and he happily responded by teaching them.

"Why not? I shall teach Krishna first. He manages to learn every step I teach in such a swift approach; I get encouraged and enthusiastic!" replied Tosha

And the boys had a petite dance tutorial in the pond. Physical energy never finds storage in small children. Young ones always focus on gaining knowledge and if molded correctly, can do wonders as they grow. Additionally the presence of Krishna added an aura which was much beyond positivity also.

Soon they were exhausted and felt hungry after the entire excursion. They decided that it was time to take lunch.

"Lunch time finally!" Madhumangala was excited.

"You all have kept me away from those lunch packs for enough of a time. Do you know that it is such a big torture to keep smelling those goodies and yet stay away from them?"

"I have to agree with you Madhumangala. Our mothers have sent us such amazing delicacies, anyone can tell with the smell itself!" said Sudama

"Mothers are embodiments of pure love. If it was not for them, no family would have survived on the planet. And that love seems to be overflowing in our lunch packs." Added on Balarama.

Aa chhaak bulaye shyam

"Come for lunch my dear friends! Called Shyam. Listening to this all the friends including Subala, Sudama and Shridama rushed together. They made plates from lotus leaves and bowls using the leaves of the palaas tree. All delicacies were served one by one in the dishes in front of the boys. Krishna, the one with the hue of a dark rain cloud, sat in the middle of the circle created by the boys and they enjoyed their lunch. Knowing that her son will be hungry in the forest, mother Yashoda packed enough lunch. Soordas's shyaam does not eat from his own plate but takes the morsels from his friends' hands and enjoys them!"

After the lunch was over, the boys lied down on the soft grass of kamyavan and began beholding the various bird species that were flying above them.

"Who can imitate the sound of a cuckoo?" said Stoka.

"Anyone but Sudama! Last time he tried to do that, he flew away all the birds!" laughed Shridama and the boys too joined in harmony.

"Don't forget the day you tried to imitate swans and ended up calling a bunch a frogs near you Shridama!" replied Sudama.

"Ok I will try this time." Said Tosha and he began to sing like the cuckoo.

Krishna couldn't help his happiness. He got up and went near him.

"My friend, we all say that you are the gandharva of vraja. But I believe that even gandharvas can be put to shame if you sing and dance. Surely, you have been born with special blessings from Lord Shiva!"

All the boys got up and surrounded Tosha. Such simplicity. There was no competition, it was just love. Love for everything they did among themselves – from being extraordinarily good to the naughtiest pranksters.

The bridge

After a while of rest, they all followed their calves and wandered around the forest. Soon they heard voices near the pond.

"O my dear companion, has it not been a difficult day for us? I am so exhausted, I simply have no energy to reach back home!"

"You are right sakhi! After resting on the banks of the pond, I cannot find myself able to get up again."

"How wonderful it would be to have a bridge across the pond! Then we could reach our homes in such a short while!"

The boys came dragging towards the pond again to find a group of maidens who were exhausted to extremity. Sweat droplets trickled from their bright but worn out faces and they appeared to be in a state of absolute despair. As futile as this physical body is, it is the main source of all achievements that one can make. Exhaustion of the physical self can be paralyzing.

"What is the matter dear Gopikas?" Asked a concerned Krishna

"O Krishna! Is it you?! Such a beautiful surprise my darling! We were on our way back home after a very tiresome day. We had to move distances today before our curds could sell. And at the moment, we feel devastated out of tiredness" said one of the gopis.

"We were just pondering our thoughts over an imaginary bridge on this pond that could allow us to reach home pretty quick!" added on the next gopi.

"Hmm! Not a bad idea. Why wouldn't I try to implement this!" replied Krishna, smiling awkwardly.

"And how do you plan to possibly implement this impossible task?" questioned a surprised cowherd maiden

Krishna spotted a high rock and jumped onto it. His appearance was heroic as ever, and this time he wanted to enlighten every living creature – that it he who has appeared before many times and in many forms for the redemption of the good and annihilation of the ghastly.

(Artist: Shuchi Mishra)

His voice, as momentous as the thunder clouds, made a declaration.

"Do you not know? That making a bridge on this mere pond is a simple game of the left hand for me! Hark! I had appeared as Shri Rama in the past eon of treta and built a bridge with the help of monkeys on the mighty ocean, joining the lands of Bharat and Lanka!"

The maidens stared in astonishment. For them, this child was one of their own – as ordinary as anyone can imagine. He might have killed the demoness Putana when he was only six days old but for them, it was the blessing of Lord Narayana that saved the little apple of their eye. He also demolished the cart by the kick of small baby foot but that was a story which every elder in vraja mandala refused to accept. He also blessed the fruit vendor a few years back by filling her fruit basket with pearls and jewels. But again, it was believed that the supreme was overwhelmed with the innocence of their little Krishna and the fruit vendor was blessed thus. Constantly convincing themselves that all miracles that had happened were not in any relation to their Krishna, they were never ready to accept that he was anything more than a simple cowherd boy of Nanda gaon.

Cowherd boys, on the other hand, were young age mates of this miraculous Govinda. For them, even the most simple thing happening was due to the prowess of their dear friend. They took pride in everything that Krishna did and strongly believed that every miracle happening was indeed performed by him. Both emotions were brimming with pure love and innocence, fusing the souls to the supreme soul and resulting in untainted bliss.

All the cowherd boys took their herding sticks and stood beside their friend and leader, shoulder to shoulder and head up.

"So our tiny prankster who goes stealing butter, pulling our hair and breaking our pots wants us to believe that he is none other than Shri Rama!?" laughed a gopika.

"Oh yes, he does. He forgets that it is us who have spared him from Yashoda's stick by restraining our complains about his mischief!" added on another lass.

"Will you not believe me – your beloved darling Krishna?" asked Krishna sheepishly.

"Not until you prove it to them dear brother. We know you can do it. Call onto Dadhilobha, he shall assist you in the task!" said an eager Balarama who had no time to waste. He was always the one to push tasks to completion before time limits.

Dadhilobha was the most notorious monkey in the territory of Vrindavana and Nandagaon. Undoubtedly, he was readily included in the group of these young boys who needed all help in performing their naughty pranks. Dadhilobha had a large network of assisting monkeys who very well gelled with the gopa kumaras of vraja. Krishna snapped his fingers in a specific manner to call for Dadhilobha and there he appeared hanging upside down from a branch of the tree just besides the pond. Just like any pets, dadhilobha was also well trained and Gopala communicated with him asking him to assist in making a bridge across the pond.

In a flash of seconds, huge groups of monkeys appeared from all four directions. Their excitement prevailed through their loud and continuous chirpings. The task begun immediately under the tutelage of Krishna. He stood on the rock with one hand on his hip and the other hand very intelligently guiding Dadhilobha about the architecture of the bridge.

Nothing could be more surprising for the maidens who saw the rocks that were placed by the monkeys float on the waters of the pond. Steadily and swiftly, the monkeys completed the bridge and assembled on the banks, looking at their hard work and feeling very proud of themselves.

"Shouldn't we reward them dear Krishna?" asked the gentle Subhadra. "They have been working very hard and have done a marvelous job indeed"

For the young boys, any miracle was never a surprise. They were very convinced that Krishna could do anything, and literally anything in the world!

Krishna nodded his head in agreement with Subhadra and looked with a side glance towards Madhumangala. Pushpank instantly understood what Krishna wanted.

"Yes Madhu! Don't shy away now! I know that you have hidden a whole bag of bananas with your lunch pack bag. You will surely share them with our dear monkey friends, won't you?" asked Pushpank.

"Well… I had planned on having them on the way back… of course I was going to share them with you all… but… anyways… ok… yes I will share them with Dadhilobha's troupe." Replied a rather guilty Madhumangala.

"We would have taken them from you anyways, if you didn't give it to them willingly!" laughed Balarama. "Let's distribute the fruits to Dadhilobha and friends! It's a joy to see them jump and dance to get the maximum fruits!"

Madhumangala brought his huge bag full of bananas and other fruit. All the boys began offering them and the monkeys created chaos around the place grabbing them. When life is natural, one does not need external reasons of laughter. Living a soulful life as exemplified by knowledgeable preceptors, gives you easy access to all laughter, contentment and happiness.

Meanwhile, the gopikas were still awestruck. They simply could not believe that this young lad who is the root cause of all havoc in vraja could actually do something so miraculuous. They tested the rocks and tried to gently step on the bridge. As Balarama saw them from a distance, he came running to them.

"Don't you think, you have doubted his accomplishments enough? Please remove all fear from your minds. This bridge has been created for your comfort and you should use it without any anxiety. At least you can trust that we will not do anything that will genuinely harm you." He said calmly to the young maidens.

They gained courage from his words and began to tread on the bridge, gradually one by one. It took their weights without any pressure and eventually the gopikas all managed to reach the other side of the pond – safe and sound. Every single one of them was spellbound, they looked at each other and could easily see that love for their darling Krishna was oozing out of everyone's eyes. Singing about his pastimes, they headed towards home.

On the other side of the pond, Dadhilobha's fruit drama had now ended. The sun had began his descent to the western mountains a while ago and it was time to return home, lest the mothers begin to worry. The boys were not going to use the bridge. One reason was that they had such large number of calves and feared that the young cows would lose their balance amidst the rush on the bridge. Secondly, they were still fully energetic. As a child, your priorities in the context of sensitivity are very different. Children will rather exercise than getting a rest and that is what makes them ever-fresh and unsullied.

The return

They boys headed towards Nandagaon. Krishna took a quicker route because he was sure that his friends will not depart to their own homes before reaching Nandamahal. He played his flute as he walked and the musical notes from his music called out the names of each and every calf. Thus, not a single calf was left behind. The gopa kumaras began to sing about his glories in accordance to the music of Krishna's flute. Joyfully, they reached a pond on the outskirts of Nandagaon. All of them refreshed by drinking water from the pond.

"You know daau, this pond was built by uncle Paavan a few years ago. He is such a pious soul – I have seen him performing so many welfare tasks around Vraja." Said Krishna to Balarama.

"Yes dear brother, and that is why he has been blessed with such a beautiful daughter– Vishakha. She is just as calm as her parents." Added on Balarama.

"Very well said daau! I will ask baba to name this pond after him. We shall call it Paavan Sarovar. It will be our token recognition for him." Krishna proposed and his brother welcomed the idea.

Bells ringing on the necks of the calves, krishna's flute, the boys singing and laughing among themselves; all the sounds together alerted the whole village that the boys have returned back. The girls' joy knew no boundaries, they all rushed to their roofs and upper balconies without delay. It had been a whole day and they had not seen Kanha! Oh, how difficult it was to pass every hour waiting for this minute.

"In the evening hours, every cowherd maiden observed was rushing to get a glimpse of him. She climbed the topmost balcony, discarding any rules and regulations set for her. As she saw him arrive amidst the huge clouds of sand that were raised by the calves' hooves, Rasikhan says that he appeared as if a large globule of smoke of striking colours had emerged from a mountain of fire!"

Eventually they reached the gates of Nandamahal. Maharaj Nanda had just returned from his duties and was exceedingly pleased to see his sons and their friends to have returned safe after performing their duties well. Mother Yashoda was on the gate of the main door. She was accompanied by all other senior ladies who knew that their sons would not head for their homes without escorting Krishna, and they too wanted to see him!

The mothers welcomed their children. It was a day of pride for them as the little ones had become slightly independent. Not only did they come back on time, but the calves appeared well herded and fed too. Listening to the tingling sounds of the bells around the necks of the calves, the cows became impatient to feed them and the calves reciprocated by ghastly rushing towards them. The senior workers handled the cowshed while the boys bid farewell for the day, with a promise to re-unite the next morning.

(Artist: Keshav Rajan, Krishna for Today)

Yashoda took Krishna and Balarama to get cleansed while Rohini laid out the supper arrangements. Maharaj Nanda arrived at the dining hall and made himself comfortable on the wooden seat carved with pearls which matched the silver low stool for placing the plates.

"Our boys seem to have done a good job today. It is good that they are getting responsible at the appropriate age." Said Rohini.

"Yes, you are correct. It was indeed good that Krishna insisted on herding. And all other boys have merrily joined in as well – I am very happy about that." Replied Nanda.

"Your broad and welcoming personality always brings out your concern for everyone together. And under your guidance, I am sure that not a single person of vraja is ever ignored in any aspect." Said Rohini as she began to serve supper.

"When a person is situated in goodness, he automatically begins to identify the good in others. And you are a perfect reflection of that!" replied a humble Nanda.

As the conversation was on, Yashoda came in with the two brothers who made themselves comfortable on either side of Nanda Maharaja and begun narrating all the happenings of the day one by one. Supper was laid out and the family enjoyed beautiful lilting moments of happiness as they honoured the food.

Slowly the moon rose right above the sky and the boys were exhausted from the day. They lay down on their silken beds and closed their lids to rest for the night as their parents admired in love.

DAY 2 – THE REDEMPTION OF BAKA
Dawn hours

As the sun rose from the Eastern skies, Vraja mandala resonated with sounds of the conches and bells together with chirping of birds, buzzing of bees and moos of the cows. Divine fragrances spread through the environment as the aroma of worship pharaphanellia, blossoming flowers and freshly churned butter combined in the atmospheric winds of the divine land.

All the gopa kumaras were well dressed and moved towards Nanda mahal to begin their routine and set out for herding the calves. They passed the temple situated just below the Nandishwara hill and the voice of a saintly being, indulged in the bliss of morning prayers, filled their ears with melody and hearts with ambrosia.

mangala aarati kar man mor, bharm nisa beeti bhayo bhor
magala baajat jhalar taal, mangalaroopa uthhe nandalaal
mangala baajat been mridang, mangala baasuri sarasa upang
mangala dhoop deep kar jori, mangala gaavati navalakisori
mangala udayo mangala raas, mangala man paramanand daas

"O my mind! Perform the auspicious morning rituals as the night representing ignorance has passed and the dawn has set in. Auspicious sounds of musical instruments such as cymbals, horns, mridang and the flute are asound as the son of Maharaj Nanda, who is the embodiment of auspiciousness, wakes up. The auspicious incense and lamps have been lit as people engage in prayers and young girls sing auspicious songs. The sun who is auspiciousness personified has risen and the heart of Paramanand das is filled with auspiciousness."

"Such beautiful early morning auras!" exclaimed Sanandana.

"And it will become more beautiful as we meet our Krishna very soon." added on Subala; as they all moved their calves towards the palace of Nanda Maharaja.

At Nanda Mahal, mother Yashoda moved towards the room of her sons while exchanging discussions with mother Rohini.

"We should wake them earlier today sister. I have called for Rangana and Rankana both to show the boys some jewellery designs that they might like. They can meet before the boys leave for herding." Told mother Yashoda to Rohini.

"Yes, I will pack their lunches while you sit with the jewelers and the boys. Rest assured my dear." assured the ever caring Rohini.

Other members of Vraja were already present by the doors of the rooms, awaiting the arrivals of the mothers so that they may enter in. People of vraja may be harsh with the choice of words but are full of love. They spoke softly so as not to startle their princes as they entered the rooms when mother Yashoda opened the ruby studded doors with pearl ornate handles. With utmost love and affection the princes were woken up. As they rose from their sleep, each member of the crowd wanted to express their love towards them. Mother Rohini entered the room and opened the curtains to allow the freshly emerged sun rays to enter the room and the brothers got out of their beds stretching their arms as if to accept all the fondness that was being over flown towards them from all directions. Everyone feasted their eyes on the beauty of Krishna and Balarama. Even though they had just woken up and had negligible adornments on, their natural splendor of messy hair, smeared eye kohl and easy smiles was enough to put a myriad cupids to shame.

"Get up boys, you must finish your daily chores quick today. Rangana and Rankana are on their way to show you some exquisite jewellery." Instructed mother Yashoda.

"Rangana and Rankana mother? Why? What's the occasion?" asked Krishna rubbing his eyes.

"Dev Deepavali is around the corner my sweet son. And since you both specially love the jewellery designed by Rangana and Rankana, I have called them so that we may tell them in advance about your choices."

"Oh yes! We get new jewellery daau! This time I'm choosing pearl decorated jewellery."

"And what makes you take that decision little one?"

"Do you remember yesterday we helped the girls cross the pond at Kamyavan? There were so many lotuses on the banks of that pond and as dadhilobha threw the rocks in the water, some droplets landed on the petals of the lotus flowers and when I went near them, they appeared as if light pink pearls were embedded on them. Oh! How pretty they looked!" Krishna gave an extended description.

"You helped the gopis cross the pond?!" asked Atulya, Krishna's aunty.

"Yes aunt Atulya, Krishna and dadhilobha built a bridge across the pond in Kamyavan!" told Kalind.

"Oh yes!" exclaimed mother Yashoda as all the elders laughed the story. They all thought that the boys were talking about a game they played. After all, who wanted to even think about bridges on a pond built by small little boys who barely managed to handle their clothes and ornaments perfectly!

"Okay, let us get going with daily chores before the jewelers arrive." Said mother Rohini.

Morning chores were completed and the boys gathered in the seating arena of the palace to wait for the jewelers to arrive. Rangana and Rankana were both jolly in nature. Anyone would laugh in their association. Plump bodies and broad smiles across their faces at all times marked their trademark of personality. The gopa kumaras always enjoyed their company as they shared so many lovable moments not only of jewellery but of a special friendship which was cultivated from jokes and fun.

Towards the forest

While waiting for them, Nanda maharaj enquired from the elder boys of the group "you must have observed the major roads and pass-ways of the forests while roaming. What route do you plan to take today for herding?"

"I have just had a word with daau, baba. We have planned to head directly towards khadiravana today and then pass through kumud vana in the afternoon and back home by evening." Responded Subhadra.

Subhadra and Balarama were the big brothers of the whole group. They made major decisions and took care of the younger ones – very efficiently. In the early days, knowledge was not bookish. Education was very practical. Practical education helped to build in character and personality in children from a young age, and helps for both material and spiritual progress. Hierarchies were built in groups of small boys and each one of them was given certain responsibilities which were exchanged and intermingled regularly. The younger children trusted the elder ones and were given love in return. Cleanliness was not only maintained physically but also mentally, keeping children deprived of hatred, competition and jealousy.

"Very good plan boys. I am very satisfied to see you taking up your responsibilities independently. Remember to keep safe and make sure the calves don't wander very deep in the forests else it will be difficult to recollect them. And yes, the elder gopas will be taking the cows straight to Govardhan today. You might cross paths with them too!" Nanda Maharaj applauded the boys.

Just then chuckles and giggles were heard from afar and the all the boys ran towards the entrance to welcome their dear Rangana and Rankana. Krishna jumped and hugged them tight. Their chubby tummies felt like soft pillows to Gopala and he loved cladding on to them. As they reciprocated the embrace of Krishna, their hearts filled with love and eyes welled up with tears of happiness, broadening their smiles even more.

They looked at Krishna and said, "My dear, even though we see you very often, every time we meet, it feels as if we have been separated from eons."

Govinda hugged them again and they all sat around discussing the jewellery. Pearl jewellery was selected for everyone following the prince's choice this time. And mother Yashoda had a conversation about the price. When honesty was predominant, there were no reasons for bargain to happen and prosperity was abundant, without exceptions.

Soon mother Rohini stepped in with servants carrying the lunch packs of the boys.

"It's time to move little boys! The calves are waiting for you and you must leave early so that you are back on time – just like yesterday. And do not forget mother Yashoda's instructions. You should abide by them daily." She said as the servants handed out the lunch packs to Subhadra and Tosha.

Eager calves led the way for the enthusiastic battalion of gopa kumaras as they made their way towards Khadiravana. Curious residents of vraja mandala gathered on the sides of the pathway to catch a glimpse of this wonderful scene of Shri Krishna along with his brother, friends and groups of calves. Bells on the necks of calves made jingling noises and the jolly little fellows danced their way towards the forests in rhythm to this sound. Notorious calves who tried to break through the group were grabbed back by the young gopas every now and then. The elders were happy and proud to see their children at their best in all sense. Thus, in all elegancy, the boys entered the peripheries of the forests.

chale braj te go charan gopa
praat samay sar kamala-khanda te janu hansani ke opa
syaam peeta pata raam neela, nata janu kaachhe sisu punja
mahuvari benu bikhan baasuri manu saaje ali gunja
tin maha nand-nandana ki sobha jyo udugan me chand
paramanand jasoda ke ghar paragate anand kand

"The crowd of cowherd boys started their journey from their residence to herd the cows. It appeared as if a large cluster of swans emerged from a pond full of lotuses in the early hours of the day. Krishna wore yellow garments and Balarama had blue garments. The tender young boys marched as if they were little dancers and the sound of different wind instruments that they played sounded like the buzzing of bees. Amidst the entire troupe, the son of Maharaja Nanda showed up like the moon amidst the stars. Paramanand das sings that bliss personified has come to the house of mother Yashoda."

The tall trees of Khadira, spreading their branches like umbrellas seemed to welcome the boys under their shades to offer some relaxation. They all settled under a tree while the calves diverged slightly to enjoy the lush greenery of the woodland. Groups of bees, birds, deers, rabbits and other fauna made the environment matchless even for paradise. Naturally singing, chirping and buzzing of the animals seemed like soothing music that generously propagated positivity and coolness all around.

(Artist: Parimala Bhakta Sohoni)

"Who can hop like the rabbit?" said Madhumangala as he sat up like a rabbit ready to take a leap.

"Be careful Madhu! Your belly is full of Kachoris made by aunt Sumukhi. You might lose balance and land directly into Sangam Kund!" laughed out Bhadrasena.

"And how do you know how many kachoris I had?" Madhumangala was slightly upset.

"Nandimukhi didi told me everything when I came to collect you and your calves this morning. In fact, aunt Sumukhi has given me a few for our lunch pack too!" replied Bhadrasena.

"And you didn't tell me that you have some more Kachoris from maa?" Madhu was even more upset now.

"Of course he wouldn't Madhu! He has to protect them!" laughed Pushpank.

Now Madhu was sulking.

"Oh! Now now, don't you all turn his mood down." Said a caring Krishna as he moved towards Madhu.

"Yes, and not like we will have the kachoris without sharing with you my dear!" added on Balarama.

"And no one hops like Madhu! Show them Madhu! You will look just like the rabbit next to Sangam kund!" said Krishna

"Why don't we all have a hopping competition and head towards the pond?" Sudama was excited.

"A fine idea indeed, but you all keep safe near the pond ok. Gobhat and I will tend the calves behind you all!" instructed the elder Subhadra and everyone abided.

It was a feast for the eyes of all divinities watching from above to see the celestial group of boys hop together like rabbits. As the omnipotent and omnipresent supreme intermingled with his love yearning souls, bliss was expanded to unlimited bounds.

The ferocious bird

In no time, they all reached the banks on sangam kund. Gobhat and Subhadra were capable enough to bring all the calves safely to the water reservoir too. Everyone quenched their thirst and enjoyed the scenery of swans swimming among clusters of lotus flowers adorned by the buzzes of bees.

Shridama noticed something quite unusual and huge on the left side of the pond. "What is that large mountain like creature on the other bank of sangam kund? I have never seen it before!"

"Indeed, I had come here just a few days back and I'm quite sure this creature was not there." Added on Tosh.

"Even my aunt had come this way last night. If this creature was here, it wouldn't have gone unnoticed – I can bet on that." Said Pushpank.

"Of course, it is very very huge to go unnoticed by anyone. It might be something we should warn our elders about." Whispered Subala.

"Yes, you are right. Should we go right away?" questioned Subhadra.

"But, what could it be? I feel afraid, we should probably move away from here immediately." Said Madhumangala.

"Absolutely boys, Krishna let's take away our calves from here. It might just be dangerous." Said Balarama as he started tending the herds away from thepond but he did not receive a reply.

"Krishna! Krishna? Are you here?" he asked inquisitively.

"Krishna, Krishna! Kanha!" added the others.

"You cannot be playing pranks at this time of danger! Where are you Krishna?" Gobhat was very serious.

"Oh Lord Narayana! Look at this giangantic bird! It has its mouth opened! It is this creature that was lying down there" said Madhumangala, very afraid.

As they turned their faces, they saw an extraordinarily huge bird standing occupying awkward length and widths. Soon they realized that Krishna was swallowed by this creature that they were discussing about so immensely that they didn't realize this mishap happening. They were all spell-bounded and their minds could not register any further action. Almost unconscious, they lost their ability to think of anything else.

Krishna was their very breath. How could this happen! No life could be imagined in vraja without Krishna. Besides, who can be so strong to gain victory over Krishna? No one. Without any second thought, there could be no one who could stand the power and potency of Krishna. So how can this mere huge bird devour him? And he did so in jiffy! Maybe it was a dream that they were going through. Maybe he was somewhere else and the bird did not harm him.

Every possible thought went through the stand-still minds of the young children. The calves also noticed that Krishna was missing and sensed that there was a danger around.

The next moment they saw that the big bird disgorged Krishna and he was on the ground. It was a sight of redemption when they saw that Krishna was totally un-harmed. Like a river flowing into an ocean, all the cowherds and calves rushed towards him but lo! In the next moment, the bird began attacking with its hefty beak. As it bent down, it felt like its whole body may land on the boys thus causing them to move backwards. They utterly wanted to reach Krishna but as soon as they took some steps forwards, the bird would bend down to attack Krishna with its beak and the boys moved back in the fear of everyone getting trampled under the bulky body of the demon.

Noticing that his friends were becoming increasingly agitated, Krishna decided to finish the game. Within the blink of an eye, he incarcerated the demon by holding the two halves of its beak in his two hands. He bifurcated the bird by stretching apart its beak just like a child splits a blade of the darbha grass. Stretching the beak beyond extreme ability, Krishna killed the demon, giving rise to showers of flowers falling from the sky.

Awestruck with all that was going on, the cowherd boys jumped around with joy on an added victory of their darling friend. They had gone through a rigorous mental turmoil upon witnessing Krishna at risk and deserved every moment of delight. Shridama lifted Krishna on his shoulders with a deep sense of happiness and pride. After all, he was the love of his sister. Every heroic deed that he performed was indeed the victory of his sister's affection for Krishna. The boys danced and jiggled around the waters of sangam kund as the calves also resorted to swimming to express their ecstasy.

The beauty of Kumud vana

"If we have all relaxed now, I think we should move forward now. I have planned to have lunch at Kumud van today. It is exactly opposite the Sangam Kund hence we will all have to move around with the whole herd." Said Balarama.

"Just a moment daau! I want to pick up some khadir leaves and twigs. They are very helpful in keeping the teeth, lungs and tummy healthy. We can store it for some days at home." said Subala.

"Such a beautiful thought dear Subala!" praised Krishna.

"And so obvious that it was YOU who would have thought of this idea." Added Madhumangala.

"Absolutely Madhu! Subala is always so thoughtful. We are lucky to have him as a friend!" Shridama additionally praised him.

"Aha! So next time we plan a prank, Subala will be leading the thought process. Ok Subala?" laughed Sudama.

Everyone knew that he was the most timid one in the entire group who kept away from all pranks and was ever absorbed in gaining knowledge. But who would leave the chance to try to entice him.

"On the other hand, I will be the one who leaks out your plans. Be careful ha!" Subala tried to be sheepish as he collected the leaves and twigs. He was not good at it and made everyone laugh.

"You will not my dear friend!" said Krishna tapping his shoulder confidently. "You won't tell anyone! Else I will not give you the new Katha Sangraha that baba has brought from the ashrama." He winked and whispered.

The boys laughed as they helped him collect the plants' parts and packed them safely into one of the side garments of Krishna. It was time to head forward now and therefore all the calves were congregated and they all began the next stage of the journey as per plan.

Singing and dancing in the wholesome bounty of nature through the lanes of the forests, they soon reached the temple of Durga Devi on the outskirts of Kumud vana. Each and every cowherd boy paid respects at the temple while the calves wandered in the shade of the large dome. The surrounding was peaceful and intimidated them to rest for a while but Balarama suggested that the calves must be getting thirsty so they better head towards Kumudini kund inside Kumud vana straight away. They all agreed and moved on further.

Fresh aromas of water flowers spread throughout the vicinity in and around Kumud vana. Nothing could be more revitalizing. Attracted by the smell of kumud flowers and slight buzzing of bees, the herd of calves moved towards the pond as if pulled by a magnet. Tingling sounds of their bells were accompanied by the music that emanated from the ornaments worn by the young lads who jogged after them for their protection.

(Artist: Chhaya Garhewal)

As they reached the banks of the ponds, the calves started enjoying the cool waters and the younger boys could not resist a perfect swim. Gobhat and Subhadra were apprehensive.

"It's time for lunch, swimming will delay. What do you say Balarama?" asked Gobhat as he stood with an eyebrow raised; looking at Balarama from the side of his eye. Everyone knew how adamant he was on maintaining timings for daily schedules. He never compromised his meal times, never delayed his morning routines and never missed out any session of exercise. And that all made him the famous body builder of the cowherd boys gang. All elders were quite unperturbed when their boys were with Gobhat, Subhadra and of course, Balarama.

"Not to worry Gobhat. Let them enjoy for some time. I will pull them out in a while. And After all, you won't let them swim after lunch, will you? You also plunge in, the waters look extremely appealing." Balarama convinced him. There was a soft portion in Balarama's heart that made him respect almost any activity of anyone. The completely represented his name – a combination of strength and pleasure giving potency.

After a while of swimming, Balarama ordered that lunch should be honored.

"Come on little ones, time for lunch now." He said

"Not so fast daau, the fun has just begun!" exclaimed Vasudaam.

"Do you know that the food our mothers pack for us is devotionally offered to Lord Narayana and given to us as his blessings? Untimely consumption of prasada is dishonoring it." Balarama explained very lovingly.

No one could withstand the warmth of Balarama and the added excitement created by Krishna.

"Yes daau is totally right. If we delay, our mothers will know at home and we will get a good shouting when we return back. There can be no better astrologers than mothers when it comes to our concern. Besides, I have so many goodies today and especially told mother to give me the fresh curd that was made by Pishangi's milk. I have lots and we will share!" Krishna encouraged further.

Pishangi was the huge dark hued cow of Nand Maharaj whose milk was super delicious. Krishna and Balarama always preferred her milk and today there was curd!

Everyone got out of the pond and dried themselves. Picking up their lunch packs, they sat around in a semi circle, surrounding Krishna who sat at the centre. Gradually, the goodies started coming out of the packs one by one and the lunch ceremony began. Krishna shared the fresh curd as he had promised and every drop of it was enjoyed to the extent that the young boys even licked Krishna's hand to obtain the ultimate taste of satisfaction.

Aaj dadhi meetho madana gopal
Bhaave mohi tiharo jhootho sundara naina vishal
Bahut divas ham rahe kumuda vana Krishna tihare saath
Aiso swaad ham kabahu na chakhyo sunu gokul ke naath
Aane paatra banaye dona diye sabani ko baat
Jinha nahi paayo suno re bhaiya meri hatheli chaat

"The curd tastes exceptionally sweet today O Madana Gopala! O our friend with large beautiful eyes, the taste of your left overs is very dear to us! We have come and resided in Kumud vana with you for many days, O Krishna! But we have never had a taste so wonderful indeed, O Lord of Gokula! Krishna brought leaves and made bowls out of them to distribute among his friends. "If anyone is left out, you can lick some from my hands" he joyfully offered. He smiled, enjoyed and delighted his friends as part of his pastimes as a commoner. Paramanand das says "O my Lord! I have recognized you well – you are the Lord of the three worlds!""

Food tastes much better when relished with loved ones. Flovours are enhanced and every morsel satisfies the body and mind as well. In the group of these boys, love was so abundant that every moment was replenishing for the minds of even those who simply watched them, spoke about them or heard about them. After the lunch ceremony, they drank the cool waters of the pond and decided to rest for a while as the calves were comfortably grazing around them within a confined periphery.

Krishna sat under a Kadamba tree facing the Sangam Kund. His elegant bluish tinted body rested on the trunk of the tree and he removed his tucked flute. Holding it in one hand, he turned his peacock feather bedecked head towards the waters and seemed to flow away with its waters. Sangam Kund – the pond of unison. It was at this spot that he enjoyed with his beloved at so many occasions. Her beauty was extraordinary – she required no adornments to compliment. When they met in the past summer, she simply wore her light cotton garments and tucked up her hair with a single pin. Slender chains and bangles decorated her body. She would never miss out on the lovely Kohl in her eyes and most beautiful in the entire universe was her smile. A smile that was augmented even more when she saw Krishna.

Oh yes! That was her! As simple as that. Krishna would wish for time to stand still even when he thought of her.

(Artist: Dr. Mukta Tripathi)

Soon the boys came along dancing and singing. They stopped at a distance when they saw that Krishna was deeply immersed elsewhere.

"What could he be thinking?" asked Pushpank

"He might be thinking of what mother is making for dinner. I heard that mother Yashoda is making special Rabri from Shyamala's milk today!" said Madhumangala.

Everyone could not help and burst out laughing.

"Everyone thinks others to be like himself only. Madhu is such a cute example." Smiled Gobhat.

"No. He is definitely not thinking about food. His smile has the tinge of love and his eyes are full of affection. He is looking for something but yet satisfied. Look carefully." explained Shridama.

"And who would recognize this better than you my dear! You are absolutely right." Balarama tapped on Shridama's shoulder.

All the boys looked at Shridama. They all knew but had no reasons to share it verbally. Strong relationships are like that.

"So should we disturb him?" asked a very concerned Subala.

"I don't want to but no games are fun without him. And I really want to play." Said a sulking Pushpank.

"Haha, don't worry you young one! He will come to play with us. We can call him." Said Balarama.

That was it. All boys needed only Balarama's permission to interrupt Krishna in any situation. They all went running towards him. It was like they dearly missed him for even those little gaps of few minutes. Krishna hugged them altogether with his huge arms.

"So what's on the list of games today?" he asked majestically.

Oh! There was a wave of excitement among the group of boys. Their Krishna was ready to play and for them nothing matched that happiness. If it wasn't for the rules of nature that their parents forced them to follow, they could play with him their entire life, continuously through the day and night, not tiring off even a bit.

"Tug of war today! I have brought my high strength rope along today!" Subhadra was enthusiastic.

"And what do the losing team have to pay?" asked Vasudaam

"The losing team will carry the winning team on their shoulders starting from the Kadamba tree to the pond." Declared Balarama.

Everyone agreed and they began their game. Krishna and Balarama usually took opposite sides to increase and maintain the passion on both sides. Having both brothers on the same would result in a significant shift in the equilibrium of enthusiasm.

Tug of war is such a practical game in this world of struggle. We all have to face opposing forces towards our aims and have to choose between applying ultimate strength to every task or simply giving up and falling down. The game began and boys pulled the rope with all the possible strength they had. Noises of names, screams and shouts filled up the environment as they continued their game. After quite some moments of resistance, Krishna's team landed up on the ground. But the chastity of kids is simply immeasurable; they simply got up giggling and were ready for the next part – carrying their opponents to the pond. Children keep life so simple with an aim to enjoy everything. If only that spirit was carried forward until adulthood, the world would make a happier home for all.

The crimson western horizon

After all the noise-making, it was time to head back home, lest the sun sets while traveling back. Very meticulously, they tamed their calves to get together from all corners of the forest and began to tend them towards home. Evening hues were beautiful as the sun headed towards the western horizon. Chirping birds were returning to their nests and lotus flowers in the waters had begun closing their petals. Flowing waters of mother Yamuna could be clearly heard now as life in general was fatigued and generally quiet during the later hours of the day.

On the lanes of vraja, the resounding bells of the calves' necks and various instruments played by the young boys as they came home struck a chord in everyone's mind, including the cows. Separated from their children for the entire day, the cows and mothers rushed to significant distances on the route of the boys and calves. It appeared as if two oceans of love flowed towards each other and got intermingled as the mothers embraced their children.

The loving procession soon arrived at the gates of Nanda Mahal. Mothers were waiting eagerly – both cows and cowherd gopikas. Their udders and breasts became swollen with the milk of love as they welcomed the children back home, drenching their clothing and clearly showcasing their affection. Hearing the strident moo-s of their mothers, the calves rushed towards the cowshed just like a small rivulet gushes towards the ocean. In the courtyard of Nand mahal, the young children were encapsulated in the hugs of their mothers and each passing second filled the environment with more love.

"You have come well in time today dear boys. The sun is just about to set and darkness has not peeped in. Very good time management!" said aunt Peevari as she caressed Subhadra's head.

"So mother, can we please stay for a little while more and play catch once?" asked an innocent Madhu.

"Sure sure. I also have to pick some special curds from sister Yashoda today. And Kushala also wanted to get some milk of Dhoosar cow for a prayer at her home. So you boys may carry on for some time while we sort ourselves." said Sumukhi as they all laughed at the impatience of the boys to play.

"But before we play, let's hand over the Khadira plants that we picked up for our homes to Baba!" said Krishna as he untied his side cloth to reveal the herbs to Nand Maharaja.

"Such a wonderful thought my dear boys! Very proud of your thoughtfulness!" said Baba Nand.

"It was Subala's idea Baba!" said an honest little Gopala.

"Aha! Subala is surely growing up to become more and more like brother Upanand – just as thoughtful!" exclaimed Nanda Maharaja as the others agreed with him.

After sorting out the lunch packs and other pharaphanellia to the servants under the surveillance of Balarama, Gobhat and Subhadra, the boys soon engaged in another playing session, creating chirping noises, laughing, fighting and running about.

Gradually, each elderly gopika began to move towards her house as other chores needed to be attended to and her son also unwillingly went along. Soon, Krishna was alone playing with Hansi – his favorite calf in the courtyard. Balarama stood on the topaz studded staircase of the entrance, he smiled and his heart swum in the confusion of love. He did not want to disturb the game and enjoyed every bit of watching Krishna. At the same time, he wanted to call Krishna to be with him.

"Rama! Why don't you call Krishna? You have already freshened up and he is still playing out. The sun has set and the courtyard is also getting dark. Nand Bhaiya will be on his way soon. Don't you all want to have dinner together?" asked mother Rohini as she passed through the scene.

"They have a special chemistry sister. Balarama will not disturb Krishna for anything. I will call him right now." Mother Yashoda gave a loving intervention.

Saanjh bhayi ghar aavahu pyare
Daurat kaha chot lagaguhe kahu, puni kheliho sakare
Aapuhi jaai baah gahi layi, kheh rahi lapatayi
Dhoori jhaari taato jal lyayi, tel parasi anhavayi
Saras basan tan pochhi syam ko, bheetar gayi lavayi
Soor syam kachhu karo biyari, puni rakho paudhayi

"It is dark now my dear son, please come inside the house. Where are you running to? Be careful lest you hurt yourself. You can play tomorrow morning again. Yashoda went forth and brought Krishna in holding his hand and noticed how he had become full of dust. She cleansed him, applied oil and gave him a bath with warm water. Wiping his body with a delicate towel, she took him inside and said come dear, have some dinner then I shall put you to sleep."

The family enjoyed dinner together and retired for the day, giving their bodies a well deserved rest so that they may be ready to for the next day.

Day 3 – The Longing of the Ladies

Wakening

Sometimes it appeared as if even the sun was in a rush to enter the land of vraja as it was distinctive in terms of all positiveness – full of energy, love and happiness. Even the gods cherished to live just a single day in this distinguished vicinity. It was the land where man created his own happiness by spreading love without discrimination of even living and non living things. And a population where people create happiness can never be deprived of anything materialistic as well.

As the red yellow orange sun rays broke through the clouds and made way through the dense forestry of vraja mandala, the waves of mother Yamuna welcomed them in her comfortable lap. Her waters made little tickling sounds that slowly woke the flora and fauna around her. Soon the animals began to respond to the dawn hours and natural alarm clocks resounded through the habitats and people regularly began to wake up from their state of sleep. Without wasting a moment of the brahma muhurta or early dawn hours all the pious souls headed towards their daily routine. For those who have realized that nothing is more important than life and nothing can be more destructive that wasting moments of that life, laziness automatically dashes away.

Nanda Maharaj arose to the chirping sounds of birds which stroke the natural clock without a second of delay. He recited the prayers to be said before getting up and then completed daily chores. Mother Yashoda also followed the same custom daily – not because it was simply a tradition but because every part of it had a science, a reason and a deeper benefit. She heard the sounds of cowherd boys twittering and humming morning ragas approach her palace and headed towards the chambers of Krishna and Balarama to wake them up.

(Artist: Priyanka Gupta)

It was quite early in the morning and all the boys were accustomed to getting up early by now. It was not a big deal anymore but just a simple errand. Because their mothers believed in the best for their children – best beyond materialism, best holistic approach towards life that made each moment fruitful. Anything in excess is harmful – even nectar. Sleep, food, comfort and entertainment are all necessary but excess can be harmful.

Praat samay bhayo rajeeva lochana, sang sakha thhade gomochana
Bikasit kamala ratata ali sreni, uthhahu gopal guhau teri beni
Kheer khaand ghrit bhojana kije, sadya doodh dhauri ko peeje
Paramanand prabhu sab sukhadaani, uthhahu gopal kahati nandaraani

"O lotus eyed one! Dawn has set in and your friends are waiting for you with their calves. The lotus flowers have blossomed and bees are buzzing around them continuously. Please wake up Gopala; I shall do your hair nicely! Take a sumptuous meal of sweet rice, condensed milk and ghee. Also, have the fresh milk of our fair cow. The Lord of Paramanand is the treasure-house of all bliss. Please wake up! Thus exclaims Nandarani Yashoda!"

A breeze of happiness flew through the hearts of all on-lookers as Krishna slowly opened his lotus eyes. Love oozed from all directions and the prince of vraja arose for the day amidst all abundance. Millions of cows made auspicious sounds, birds chirped away in pleasure, the sun rays decorated the courtyard in shades of yellow and sounds of curd churning was coming from all directions. Krishna got up and entered the arms of mother Yashoda. He felt contented and energized as he received the warmth of her hug. All the other ladies, men and children showed their love in various ways too. Balarama noticed that if this was to continue, they might have to cancel their herding today because once exchange of true love begins; there are no measurements of time. He slowly drifted away from the room and blew his horn loudly creating a delightful buzz that helped in everyone to come out of the loving trance.

"That's daau's horn! As majestic as himself, isn't it friends?" said Krishna getting up from his bed.

"No doubt! All his deeds and his pharaphanelia are just as majestic as himself. My idol for lifetime. I aspire to be just an atom of what he is!" replied a mesmerized Gobhat, staring reverently towards the direction from which the sound of the horn was coming.

"Come come, move on. You have to follow him to be like him. Get up!" said Subhadra as he held Gobhat's hand towards the door.

"And everyone move on as well. Time is passing. You must go on time so that you return well on time before the sun sets." said mother Rohini.

And the group of people slowly dispersed towards their waiting duties from the grand chambers of Krishna and Balarama. It appeared as if droplets of ambrosia were leaking out of a gem studded pot. The boys and men headed towards the cowshed to give the calves a good feed before they leave for the forests. Mothers and ladies headed towards

the kitchen to arrange for the lunch of the boys. Krishna and Balarama
went on to complete daily chores.

One by one, everyone got together and general instructions were given
to the boys. Although these instructions were summoned daily, it never
felt to be monotonous to the boys. They overheard them each day
anticipating their entire day on the basis of what was being told. If
reciprocation is positive, then relationships last longer.

The ladies handed over lunch packs to the boys. Healthy sumptuous
foodstuffs were packed lovingly for the boys each day. Bunches of
fruits, freshly cooked savories and all time favorite curd rice were
necessities each day. All the boys distributed the foodstuffs to be
carried according to age and strength. They began their journey with
the melodious sound of Krishna's flute. He started off after the cows
and the cowherd troupe followed next.

The day without him

All spectators looked upon without blinking on the path of their
departure until the last speck of dust flew from the footsteps of the
cows and gopas. As if enjoying every atom of the presence of their
beloved Krishna, they stood in a trance and enjoyed every portion of
the echo from his flute. When nothing was visible or audible, the spell
broke and finally their limbs started moving. The elder gopas headed
towards their duties of herding the bigger cows, maintaining the
cowsheds, collecting dairy and working in the farms. The ladies also
moved on to their daily chores, while lovingly murmuring about
Krishna and his friends.

Mother Yashoda and mother Rohini headed towards the kitchen.
Other servants went on to handle their respective duties in the palace
of Nanda Maharaj. What can be said about the beauty of this palace?!
From decades ago, this residence has been decorated with the good
deeds and devotion to Narayana by the family of Nanda. As a result,
this palace has never experienced scarcity of anything. Since the birth

of his son, Nanda Maharaj has himself acknowledged that there has been special abundance. Milk and dairy would flow from the kitchen, gold and silver would not fit into the treasure boxes, the servants were extremely elated at all times and the gardens were always filled with fruits and flowers.

"Nirmala! Sumukha and Ranjan will be here in a while. Please remember to give them the clothes of Krishna Balarama that are supposed to go for wash!" mother Yashoda raised her voice to servants attending Krishna's room.

"Yes mother, we have removed them aside." came back a loud reply.

"Nirmala, I have collected the stale flowers from the room. As always, not even one of them has withered off. We can arrange them outside the cowshed. The cows will enjoy a scented breeze through the day. What say?" said Ujjwala who was assisting Nirmala in decorating the chambers of the princes.

"Very well said, dear! These flowers have become even fresher after receiving the aroma emanating from our princes bodies! Oh! They actually do not even need any adornments – be it flowers or jewellery. They are self adorning, naturally beautiful and ever-fresh, isn't it?" replied Nirmala.

All members of the palace, be it queen Yashoda or her servants or even the animals, passed the entire day purely waiting for Krishna to return in the evening. For the day, they passed each moment discussing various instances and characteristics related to him, thus being mentally attached to him despite the physical separation.

"Sister Ujjwala, hopefully you are not late in cleaning the room today. Sumukha and I are in great hurry. Maharaja Nanda has instructed us that the curtains in the courtyard and covers of the cowshed need to be washed. Please give us the clothes from the palace!"

Ujjwala and Nirmala came running out with the clothes hearing the voice of Durlabha.

"Ranjan didn't come today, brother?" asked Ujjwala as she handed over the clothes to him.

"He is busy in the cowshed, pulling down the covers. Maharaja Nanda said that the boys will be learning how to milk the cows tomorrow and therefore everything needs to be decorated. We will be returning back to arrange new covers and curtains and will bring back these clothes washed up for you." Durlabha, the main washerman of the family, was indeed in a hurry and intended to complete all tasks as assigned by Nanda Maharaja well in time.

"Just a second brother! Mother Yashodaaaaa! I have handed over the clothes for wash, is there anything you want to give. They are in a hurry, come soon!" shouted out Nirmala.

"Coming coming! You loud little chatterbox! How far is the kitchen? Can't you come and ask me?" Mother Yashoda chastised her lovingly. Her servants were like her own children.

"Sumukha, here is my Banarasi shawl. It is messed up with curd. Please handle it with care while washing."

"How did so much curd spill on your shawl mother?" asked a surprised Nirmala.

"Oh! It was yesterday at the dining area. I was sitting in between the two brothers who were teasing each other all along dinner. As Balarama made his face to mock Krishna's mouth gasping at the fresh butter I served, Krishna wanted to reply while holding his bowl of curd. In the process of poking his brother, he dropped the whole bowl on me. Ujjwala was there, remember dear!" said mother Yashoda.

"Oh yes mother! They both cause such fun when they are around. The day seems heavy without them." Ujjwala replied in a fading voice.

"Not really sister! Their memories fill up the gap, isn't it? Aren't we all rejoicing in their sweet pastimes day and night?" Durlabha opted to answer quick. Everyone nodded in acceptance.

"Let's go now. Maharaja Nanda will be waiting for us. See you all in the evening!" Sumukha interrupted so that work could be attended to.

"Alright my dears, just make sure that the rooms are cleaned, mopped, dusted and decorated. Krishna spoke a lot about the lotus flowers from ponds yesterday. Take a look outside near Vrinda Kund, collect the lotus flowers and arrange the room of the boys with them. They will be very happy." Mother Yashoda gave instructions as she walked towards the granary.

"We will pass through Hau Bilau to go to Vrinda Kund, as the rains are almost gone, the road will not be muddy" said Ujjwala.

"Mother, is our Krishna still afraid of Hau Bilau?" chuckled Nirmala

"Balarama has totally overcome the fear but Krishna is still in between, sometimes he does get afraid! Oh! That Hau Bilau has played a special role in bringing up the boys, I must say!" Yashoda answered and all the gopis began laughing with her.

(Hau Bilau, Courtesy: a108.net)

Hau bilau is an awkward looking statue which is located on the banks of Yashoda Kund in Nandgaon. Mother Yashoda used to threaten her little boys to complete chores and tasks lest Hau Bilau comes and takes them away.

"Subhaga! Are you in the courtyard? I can hear birds chirping. Can you make sure they do not take a huge feed off the millet that I have laid out to dry?" Mother Rohini spoke as she came out of the kitchen.

"Yes mother! I am here. Krishna's plate had a few morcels left over. I have put them here and all birds are feasting from there. The millet is untouched, please don't worry." replied Subhaga as she carefully broomed the stairs of the courtyard, decorated with gems.

"Very good! As the winter is setting in, it is important that we increase the consumption of millet in our meals. Especially as they boys are out the whole day, it will protect them by keeping warm from within. Okay, I am heading towards the Brahmin hermitage. The boys will start milking cows from tomorrow. I am going to enquire if any special pooja needs to be performed and if any items need to be collected. This will help in warding off the evil eye from our children. Please inform Yashoda."

Gathering of the elder ladies

Mother Rohini walked out of the palace with two attendees as Subhaga reciprocated to her loving directives. Just as she stepped out, Sumukhi, Vatsala, Mitra and Kapila came inside along with other elder gopikas.

"Is Yashoda in, Subhaga?" asked Sumukhi.

"Yes aunty, she just went into the kitchen. You may follow!"

As they all went into the kitchen, they noticed that their friend Yashoda was busy in making butter, all the while humming in tune singing about Krishna's pastimes.

baal vinod gopal ke dekhat mohi bhaave
prema pulaki anand bhaaari jasomati gun gave
bal samet ghan saavaro aangan dhaave

"These naughty deeds of Gopala enchant my heart. With all the love and happiness, Yashoda sings about them too. He runs about in the courtyard with his brother Balarama and enters into the laps of his mother-like gopikas. That personification of bliss, who is unattainable by even Shiva and Brahma, rejoices upon seeing the smiling faces of the gopis."

(Artist: Keshav Rajan, Krishna for Today)

They all smiled in unison as they witnessed this pure love for Krishna overflowing around mother Yashoda and called out to her,

"Yashoda! Look over! We have brought so many delicacies for our little Krishna!"

Mother Yashoda looked up and welcomed them.

"Oh! Sumukhi! Kapila! Come in sisters. Such a pleasure to have you all."

"We have made rasa malai, shrikhand, laddoos and dry fruit delicacies. Please keep them aside for our princes."

"You will all spoil him together, I must say! Isn't it too much for a day?"

"No dear! No one feels satisfied with any delicacy unless tasted by Krishna. Please have them. We make these savouries for our children to enjoy, isn't it? And your Krishna is definitely the darling of each and every house of Vraja! So please store them well for him!"

You have reached an exceptional level of satisfaction when your surroundings are all your friends. There is no one to fight with, no one to compete with and no one to complain about. When one rises above all these bondages, he or she automatically frees the mind of all anxiety.

The goodies were stored and the ladies moved to relax in the hall.

"Shobha, please take the curds from the inner storeroom and prepare lassi for your aunties. Bring it in the hall when you are done!" mother Yashoda requested her helper in the kitchen and moved out with the ladies.

As the ladies gathered in the hall with cooling walls and sparkling pillars, their conversations were centered towards only Krishna. They probably did not even realize when they drank up the lassi brought in by Shobha in no time. It seemed as if his memories were the sole support of these loving ladies of Vraja as they spent an entire day without him. Since he was the supreme and all the souls present in the vicinity of vraja were previously cleansed through penance, there was a natural attraction of everyone for Krishna. The soul in its purest state is unsurprisingly attracted to the supreme and this situation was personified in Vraja!

"I wonder where the boys have taken the calves today!" exclaimed Sumukhi.

"Yes, sometimes I fear that they will wander away too far, but then I remember that Balarama is with them and will guide them properly. Although he may be just a few months older than the others, there is a comfort level that I experience when he is with Krishna." said mother Yashoda.

"You are absolutely right, Yashoda! He has completely imbibed his mother's qualities! But I wonder where our mischievous little Krishna has imbibed his mischief from!" laughed out Kapila

"Oh yes! You and Nanda Maharaj both are calm! But Krishna is different, different from all. He is special, even in his mischief. He as a whole is just astonishing! Probably there is some quality of his which beyond our thoughts but easy to experience! So much of love flows from my heart involuntarily when I see him!" Vatsala was flowing away with words…

"True to each word are your feelings, Vatsala! Even when he has the least adornments on, his beauty attracts every living and non living existence around us!" added Sumukhi.

And thus their conversation continued. Each one spoke of Krishna and his qualities as she had experienced personally.

"O Yashoda! We ward off the evil eye from your son's beautiful form! Wearing a musk tilaka and neck ornaments, his smile makes his face even more adorable! His hair is curly and decorated with tusk pearls, the damsels would give up their life on the beauty of Nand nandana. He wears yellow garments and is the Lord of Vraja. Even Lord Brahma and Lord Shiva are astonished to see his activities and beauty!"

They expressed love for him in their own special ways.

(Artist: Tista Tiwari)

"Were you making something special today Yashoda?" asked Kapila

"Oh yes dear sister! Our Dhoosar cow has given birth to a beautiful calf last month. When I met sister Kirtida last month, she mentioned to me that Radha cherished the milk of Dhoosar and would love to use it for the Soorya pooja this month. I had made curds using Dhoosar's milk last night and prepared some butter this morning. When she was milked today morning, I condensed the milk and made some sweets for dear Radha. I am planning to send the butter, sweets and a separate pot of milk for her today." replied Yashoda.

"Oh! That's lovely dear, Radha is such a darling; her love towards all of us makes us feel as if she were our own. And I must say that her divinity surpasses Krishna's!" said Kapila.

"Definitely! She is divine, more of a Goddess among us. Her presence elites my Krishna and for me, that is all that matters. I can worship her day and night for the happiness she brings to my boy! Kirtida and brother Vrishabhanu are pious souls to have begotten her!" spoke Yashoda as tears of joy choked up her throat.

"Who are you sending Yashoda? Nandimukhi plans to go towards Barsana along with Indulekha. They were planning to pick Chitra on the way too. I think they are all getting together to prepare for Dev

Deepavali. I can tell Nandimukhi to carry it with her attendants when she goes." offered Sumukhi.

"That will be great! You please send her to me with her friends and I will pack the goodies. The butter needs to be wrapped well in cool damp clothing lest it melts on the way." said Yashoda.

With utmost contentment and gladness, the elder gopikas took leave and headed out towards their residences while still having Krishna in their minds and hearts.

Conversations of the young damsels

Nandimukhi picked up the delicacies with her friends from mother Yashoda and began her journey towards Barsana. She met Indulekha and Chitra on the way. Laughter and happiness prevails when girls meet in positivity. It is heaven on earth where young girls gather together in friendship.

They took the shortcuts, the better and more pleasing option, to Barsana. The soft muddy roads were as soft as silk and leveled to uniformity by an unperturbed nature, canopies formed from creepers which seemed to be distributing their goodness to the neighboring trees as well and the comforting sounds of birds seemed to be just enough to echo the gardens that were enclosed by shrubs and bushes. As the girls laid their legs on the carpets formed by flowers on the path, their minds drifted towards their beloved too.

"Indu! It seems like Krishna has been on this path very recently. For no other reason would have these trees dropped heaps and heaps of champa and dahlia on the pathway!" said Chitra.

"I was thinking the same thing dear friend! His touch itself is enough to exfoliate the entire nature! Do you see that Kadamba tree to your left? A few days ago, I happened to catch Krishna playing his flute there and trust me, I was so much taken away that I probably traveled to another world for some moments!" replied Indulekha.

"Yes sister! It happens each and every time Krishna plays his flute! Sometimes I actually wonder how Madhu and the other boys are able to maintain their calm as they spend their whole day with him as he plays his magical flute!" said Nandimukhi

They began to share their intimate feelings in all love and reverence.

bansi tribhangi laal ki, ma meen ki banasi
kaha antar ghar duri rahe, chhai moorati ghanasi
hari dekhe bin kyo rahe dheeraj nahi tanasi
jai shri bhatt hari ras bas bhayi, suni dhuni nek bhanasi

"The flute of the curved lad! It has become a fishing hook for our minds which are attracted to it like fish! When his dark hued form appears in our hearts, it becomes unbearable to be far from him. Without catching a glimpse of him, it is not possible

to keep calm. Shri Bhatt ji says that by slightly hearing the sound of his flute, all the gopikas have become enslaved to him!"

When trust is a natural trait, conversations happen without restrictions and when conversations are honest, the mind finds contentment. Immersed in the joy of this contentment, constantly pondering over their beloved, the gopis reached Barsana.

"Aunt Kirtida! Radha! Where are you, see we have arrived! And we have lots of surprises for you, come come, take a look!" shouted the girls as they entered the bejeweled palace of King Vrishabhanu.

Mother Kirtida came out to welcome the little girls who had arrived at her palace and it seemed as though a stream of love was going to merge in the ocean of joy. She walked up in haste and clasped all the twinkling gopikas into her warm embrace. Radha came running from behind and also soaked herself in the same cuddle. A true mother's loving embrace can factually absorb the entire universe and yet have space.

"Welcome my beautiful friends! How are you all? And what surprise have you brought today?" said an innocent voice of the ever-welcoming Radha.

"We have been instructed to pass on these to you by Aunt Yashoda. She has specially collected milk from Dhoosar and made some butter for your next Soorya pooja. And for you, Aunt Yashoda has exclusively made condensed milk sweets and packed an extra pot of milk to enjoy! Here aunty, please have them stored properly." said Nandimukhi.

"Indeed, we have taken paramount care in order to bring these parcels to you dear!" said Chitra as she unloaded the pots.

"Such a beautiful gesture by my dear sister Yashoda! I shall personally thank her when we meet for the pooja of Lord Shiva at Ambika Van next month. She always has Radha on her mind and we are lucky to receive her blessings in multifarious ways!" mother Kirtida was overwhelmed with the love that her darling daughter was being showered with.

"Radha, please take your friends to the inner chambers. You can all discuss your festival plans there. Your other friends are on the way and will join you shortly."

The girls lovingly walked together, chatting and murmuring among themselves; filling the environment with a extraordinary energy of cheerfulness and ecstasy.

"O Radha! When are you going to meet Krishna again? You must request him to play raga Bageshree on his flute. It has been ages since I heard it from him and he does not listen to anyone else other than you for instructions on ragas!" said Indulekha as she sat down.

(Artist: Shuchi Mishra)

"His Bageshree is ultimate bliss! My heart overflows with emotions whenever I hear it." exclaimed Lalita as she entered the room with the other friends.

"Yes, I remember I asked him to play it last time at Vanshi Vat! Each and every moment of that melody is still fresh in my ears and heart!"

said Radha who was being absorbed in her beloved's memories. "But today, I am craving for his Tilanga!"

And eventually all the girls jumped into the conversation, releasing their feelings about Krishna's flute.

"His flute is a magician! Or is it him! Have you seen that even the stones begin to melt when his flute is asound? Have you seen that even the damsels of Indra's court descend above the skies of Vrindavana to hear his flute?"

"Yes! Adorned in forest flowers and a peacock feather in his hair, he embodies millions of cupids and as he plays his flute, the creepers, plants, trees and shrubs begin to move as if dancing in intoxication of his music and beauty!"

"I have witnessed the waters of Yamuna solidify upon hearing his flute. I was so immersed in the music that I only realized this after quite some time. Indeed, he has the ability to convert the movable to immovable and vice versa!"

"Are we not proof personified of his magic?"

"Yesterday, I happened to pass by the Kumudavana where he was grazing the calves. As he played his flute, I saw the cows, deers, peacocks and birds gaze at him with so much intensity that they all appeared to be paintings instead of living beings!"

"We are lucky to be associated with you, dear Radha! You own the heart of Krishna and we shall always find him through you!"

puni puni kahati hai braj naari
dhanya bada bhaagini radha tere bas giridhaari
dhanya nand kunar dhanya tum dhanya teri preeti
dhanya dou tum naval jori koka kalani jeeti
ham vimukh tum kirhsn sangini pran ik dvai deha
ek man ek buddhi ik chit duhuni ek saneha

"The gopis say again and again – you are great, dear Radha, as Giridhari is under your control. Blessed is the son of Maharaja Nanda and blessed are you! Blessed is the love shared by you and blessed are you as a couple! We tend to wither away from him but you are his eternal consort, one life but two bodies! You minds, intellect and hearts are one! Without having a glimpse of you, Shyam becomes restless. He repeatedly calls out your name in his flute! You have recognized him and owned over him. Soordas describes that his Lord can be defeated by true love!"

(Artist: Dr. Mukta Tripathi)

The surprised encounter

Just as they were busy in their discussions, they heard heartwarming sounds of the flute coming from a distance. They all stopped their sentences mid-way and gasped in surprise…. It was Krishna! For sure, there could be no one who could have snatched their attention within micro seconds! All the gopis rushed to the windows of the palace, the sounds confirmed that he was definitely going to pass through the pathway right below the palace.

"Oh Radha! Guess the raga? Tilanga! Oh how accurately can your thoughts match? Amazing are you both!" shouted Lalita as the flute sounds' volume increasingly became evident.

Unhurriedly, the troupe came nearer to the palace. On the way, all the residents of vraja, including the animals, shed warm gazes on their darling Krishna. They cursed the nature of the body as their eyelids fell in between and interrupted their vision. Krishna glanced at each one, without missing anyone, and filled their hearts with even more love.

ye akhiyaa jaadu bhari teri shyam
dekhi dekhi chhavi manmohan ki, mohat braj ki bam
ban te aavat murali bajavat sang liye balram
raag tilang madhura dhuni gaavat braj vanita sukhdham
bansi ki dhuni sunat magan bhai bhool gayi sab kaam
shyam teri surat pe bik gayi bina mol ke daam
kunj nikunj sudharas barasat bheejat sab braj gaam
hari ganesh hari naam lakhayo amal alaukik thaam

"Your eyes, Oh Shyam, are full of magic! Looking lovingly upon the gorgeous form of Manmohana, the gopis oof vraja are endlessly spell-bound! He comes from the forests, playing his flute, together with Balarama. The abode of happiness of the gopikas sweetly sings and resounds the Tilanga raga. As the sound of the flute reached their ears, they pardoned all other jobs. Oh Shyam, they have sold themselves to you eternally, without the price of a single penny! As the gardens and orchards get blanded with the ambrosia of love; the land of vraja shines resplendently. Hari Ganesh sings that he has the fortune of beholding this divine land through the names of Shri Hari!"

Loving exchanges were communed from both sides in so many ways that even the best of poets will not be able to do justice through description. Krishna made sure that his beloved's smallest desires were fulfilled, even if they were momentarily apart. Blushing in the very thought of this commitment, she drank his beauty with her eyes. As he moved ahead, they exchanged innumerable discussions of love just by their glances. Appreciating each other, they felt satisfied to the core. Radha closed her eyes, as if to take Krishna with her sight into her heart and lock him in there.

(Artist: Tista Tiwari)

Home for the day!

"Barsana was not planned to be enroute our way home, was it Daau?" asked an innocent Pushpank.

"It wasn't dear! But some unplanned sessions end up being the most enriching!" said Balarama as he cast his side glance towards Krishna.

"And Sridama was in a hurry today, didn't you see? Wasn't it a good idea to frop him over first today daau?" said Krishna, concealing his true intentions.

"Ok, ok! Very well done! We all understand and totally agree Krishna!" said Subhadra.

"Subala! Madhu! Sudama! Make sure the calves don't diverge into the gardens from the back side. I am handling the front end with Subhadra.

Go on Krishna, Nandgaon is still distant from here. Let's move on." said Gobhat as he gathered the calves.

The team began the journey back home. As the flute of Krishna slinked through the dense fauna of the pathway, it slowly began to echo in the ears of the mothers who were eagerly awaiting the arrival of their dear sons. Preparations began to welcome the boys. With enthusiasm and love going together, every activity is transformed into a festival.

Soon, the resonance of the flute became clearer, the sounds of boys singing and tending the calves were heard now, the tingling of the neck bells of the calves became louder and finally the mothers could view huge clouds of dust being raised by the hooves of the calves.

As Krishna entered the palace of Nanda Maharaja, all boys were welcomed by warm hugs, kisses and showers of love from their mothers and aunties. The cows came running out of the sheds to lick their offspring and the men carefully managed the herds. Servants were ready on the spot to receive the empty lunch packs, soiled clothing and accessories from the boys.

"Did you have a good day boys? What makes you early today?" asked mother Yashoda as she dusted off the soil from the bodies of Krishna and Balarama.

"Yes mother! Someone special was awaiting my arrival elsewhere so I had to be there on time!" replied Krishna.

"Oh! I see. How committed have you become, you naughty prankster. Attending to special people's anticipations!" laughed Yashoda as she caressed her boy.

Happiness upsurged among the gopis, gopas, bala gopalas, cows and calves as the day quietly came to an end, as if hinting of fatigue from all the love flowing through the day.

Dawn dazzlings

As dawn broke in vraja and the sun rays squeezed through the dense forestry, ultimately reaching the pure sands of the land, every speckle sparkled in the anticipation of the forthcoming excitement in the association of Krishna. Vraja, the exquisite terrain of genuine pleasure which emanated from chaste love for the supreme, appeared to be even more attractive as the vermillion red aura of the rising sun painted the vicinity.

As people began rising to complete their daily chores, temples resounded with bells and the chanting of young Brahmin boys echoed in the environment. The wind carried with itself these virtuous sounds and filled everyone with more energy.

Mother Yashoda walked towards the chambers of Krishna and Balarama. Their rooms still smelt fresh with the flower decorations done the evening before. The gems on their beds dispersed bright shines as they were hit by the sun rays. Servants and assistants got to their work and Yashoda walked forward to wake up her children.

mohan jag hau balgai

tere karan shyamsundar nayi murali layi

gvaal baal sab dvaare thadhe ber ban ki bhayi

gaiyyan ke sab bandh chute dagar ban ko gayi

peet pat kar door much te chhad de alasayi

ati anandita hota jasumati dekhi dyuti nita nayi

jage jangam jeev pasu khag aur braj sabahi

soor ke prabhu daras dije arun kiran chhayi

"O Mohana, arise! It is getting late! Look over, I have bought a new flute for you. All the young gopas are standing at the door as it is time to go to the forest. The cows have been freed and taken to graze. Please take away the bright sheets from your face and give up your laziness. Yashoda is delighted beyond borders to observe a fresher look of her son each day. All the lands, people and animals of vraja have

awaken, O Lord of Soordas, show us your beautiful form as the red sun rays have spread all over!"

Joy arose from all corners as Krishna lifted his eyelids and stretched his arms. Cheers, chippers and glittery faces from all directions were aimed at Krishna's face – ever green, ever youthful and ever fresh. Even with the kohl spread all over his cheeks from his eyes, he appeared to be the most handsome of all living beings. As loving exchanges took place, the day moved forward and Krishna and Balarama both got dressed. Mother Yashoda found ultimate bliss in dressing up her little lad, while the boys assisted with her requirements. Saranga quickly brought Krishna's clothes, Sumana had the flower ornaments ready and Madhukanth stood prepared with the flute and herding stick.

(Artist: Dr. Mukta Tripathi)

The presence of numerous servants could not shed even a micro-fraction of laziness on the residents of vraja when it came to attending Krishna. Everyone wanted to do everything for him. And this is the secret behind the stagnant and striking bliss of the land – even to this day.

karat shringar maiyya mana bhavat

"Mother dearly dresses up her Krishna with various embellishments. She warms up water and bathes him after putting body scrub. She uses a thin muslin cloth to dry his body and tells him 'Look my little one, how beautifully your friends are dressing and coming from their houses! Wear your yellow garments and I shall decorate your eyes with kohl and forehead with tilaka' Soorda describes that as Krishna plays in the courtyard, mother Yashoda wards off the evil eye and experiences great pleasure."

Maharaja Nanda walked in the dressing room and the young boys including Krishna and Balarama ran up to hug him. A fatherly hug is the limit of sympathy – sympathy that is craved by the child inside every human. His arms extended and spreaded love for all the boys.

"Krishna! your peacock feather is left behind dear. Come, let me fix it for you!" said mother Yashoda realizing that Krishna ran away in between the dressing session.

"Bring it Yashoda, I will do it." Maharaja Nanda asked for the feather.

"Do you know how elegant my son looks with a peacock feather! It completes his dressing and compliments his beauty!"

Maharaja Nanda fixed the peacock feather and spoke further.

"Listen you all young lads of vraja! Today is a special day as you will be learning how to milk the cows. We shall all go to the cowshed immediately. The Brahmins have already assembled there. Dhiman and Chatura have welcomed them and seated them. We must all go and offer respects, and then we shall worship the cows. And which cow would you like to begin your milking lessons on Krishna?"

"Dhoosar! Without a doubt baba! She has given us one of the most beautiful calves last month!" shouted Krishna in excitement.

"Okay Okay! Let's go then. Follow me boys."

Milking the four legged beauties of vraja

All the elder gopas, Kapila, Supaksha, Shankara and many others, accompanied Maharaja Nanda who was trailed behind by the huge team of passionate boys. The ladies followed them as if to contain the excitement with their solemn natures.

"Sumukha, Ranjan and Durlabha have decorated the cowshed so beautifully Krishna! All the curtains and shades look very nice. Mother Cows will be happy today and will not resist us milking them!" said Madhumangala as he threw his sight all over the shed.

"Aha! Yes! The shed looks like it is new!" added Pushpank

"Last evening I saw them busy decorating. Sister Ujjwala mentioned that they had taken the responsibility of cleaning and maintaining the cowshed as per baba's instructions. And they have done a fabulous job! Baba, you must give them some milk from my first pot today!" said the ever-loving Krishna.

(Artist: Keshav Rajan – Krishna for today)

Everyone was pleased. When love has a tinge of innocence and simplicity, it becomes even more beautiful. Brahmins were given respect by all members of vraja and the worship was completed. Krishna called out to mother Yashoda.

"O Mother! Please hand over the golden pot to me, Baba is going to teach me how to milk the cows. Krishna sat beneath the cows and held the udder of the cow in his hands. Hinting of initial experience, the milk flow was not straight and moved out of the pot. Maharaja Nanda lovingly laughed at the sight. All the gopikas came to watch this ceremony and became enchanted at krishna's smile. As the rituals were completed, Brahmins were given ample alms and the darling Lord of Paramanand continued to shed streams of bliss."

Yashoda ensured that the Brahmins were fed well and bid them farewell after the ceremony. Maharaja Nanda spoke to Subhadra, Gobhat and Balarama.

The glitters of Govardhana

"Boys! It is late now as the rituals took time to be completed. So, today you should only take the calves to graze on Govardhana. Take them in the valley of the hill and let them wander there. You should go straight to Govardhana, spend the day there and come back soon."

"Okay Baba! Govardhana is our all time favorite." replied Balarama.

"Govardhana – just the name fills the heart with peace, isn't it Baba? How special he is to all of us! When we walk in his valley, the creepers hanging from the trees appear to be offering their flowers on to him! His green grassy valleys and pathways make sure that our feet feel carpeted throughout our journey, the tickling sounds of his minor waterfalls fill the mind with music and the birds in his valley appear to singing in rhythm with this sound. I don't think there would be any place similar in the whole world!" Tosh gave a very vivid description.

"Who would want to see any other part of the world after seeing Govardhana! He is the ultimate amalgamation of holiness, peace, delight and nature at its best. And your poetic description just portrayed him right my dear friend!" said Sudama.

"Krishna also loves his valleys. His tranquility is mesmerizing! Shall we move then?" asked Subhadra as he and Balarama untied the calves from their pegs.

"Yes please! No time is enough to play at Govardhana. Let us all quickly unfasten all the calves!" said Krishna as he jumped into the shed and the others followed him.

"We shall touch the outskirts of Barsana and then reach Govardhana via Kamai, is that okay boys?" said Gobhat as he planned the journey.

"Very well planned Gobhat! Keep up your good work and take care of everyone. I shall now be moving to deal with the farming issues and help the dairy products sorting for sale. Have a good day my boys! Come home soon!: Maharaja Nanda encouraged the gopas as he walked away discussing many other things with the elder folklore.

Soon the troupe of gopas and calves was on their way to Govardhana. Goverdhana was an all-time favorite of all residents of vraja. With his high peaks touching the heavens hinting about his grandeur, he still seemed to be loving enough to welcome everyone by laying out a lush green carpet of fine soft grassy lands. Water streams, flocks of birds and deers, monkeys chirping on his trees, beautiful rocks just rightly placed and constricted rays of the gems embedded in his minute caves; all made him nature's epitome of beauty.

As the boys entered his locality, the calves ran hither and thither on his grassy graze lands. Owing to his intellectual mind, Subala began looking amidst the shrubs. He was specifically looking for the Malati flowers. His legs brushed across the soft green grass and got wet as the dew was not yet completely dried as yet. As he tried to jump over a row of small shrubs, it was natural for him to slip, but luckily he landed on Madhumangala. Madhu fell to the ground bearing Subala on him. Dadhilobha laughed. He was a competitor with Madhu. No opportunity was left over to mock Madhu by Dadilobha. After all, it was Madhu who was eating half his share of fruits almost every day!

The two boys got up and dusted off themselves.

"What were you doing Subala? Trying to copy Dadilobha? I have told you so many times that these games are not for you! You sit down and read books!" said Madhumangala as he removed the leaves stuck on Subala's head.

"Whatever he was doing, it's good that HE fell on YOU. If it was the other way round, you would have turned him into mashed potatoes by now!" said Pushpank carefully rubbing his hands over the chubby belly of Madhumangala.

All the boys laughed loudly as Madhu frowned.

"Leave my tummy alone you naughty fellow!" Madhu screamed as he tried to catch Pushpank who went running around the valley.

"Let's have a swing session dear friends! The tamarind tree branch seems just good in position. It is welcoming us for a swing!" Tosha proposed.

"Absolutely! These splendid creepers will do just right to make our swing, they are strong enough." Shridama agreed as he examined the creepers hanging from the tree.

"Madhu and Pushpank, boys, please look for a suitable wooden track and bring it for our swing." Krishna called out to the boys.

Within minutes, the swing was ready, strong enough to bear at least four boys in a go. Experience and practicality are probably the best methods of education; which is the reason why these young boys were efficient and independent at such a raw age. When bargaining with Mother Nature is done within limits, she happily provides not only necessities but also leisure facilities. Greed does no good, whether among ourselves or with nature.

They took turns on the swing. Sometimes willingly and sometimes through pushing and fighting for space on the swing.

Soon they heard pretty sounds.

"Hey! Those are swans for sure! Let's go have a look at them!" said Sudama.

"But let's get the calves too, the water reserves are very close to the hill. The calves will wander away behind us in the valley." instructed Subhadra.

"The swans will move away by then!" exclaimed Vishal.

"No they won't! Go ahead Krishna! Run to the hill and play your flute! Hold them while we bring the calves" said Balarama very brightly.

"Aha! What a great plan dau!" said Gobhat as he ran to collect the calves.

"I'm going ahead then! You all bring the calves near Govardhana! This season is full of swans as the rain has just subsided. They will be many around there. Be quick my friends, I will be at my task there." Krishna shouted as he ran towards the hill.

It was pure ambrosia for the eyes, drenching the soul in bliss as the boys accumulated on the foothills of Govardhana, minding their cows, watching the swans, playing with nature and listening to Krishna's flute.

giri par khelat giri ke rai
sakha mandali Madhya manohar murali madhur bajai
phool phal sakala vrindavan gunjat madhupa lubhai
kuhu kuhu bolat mor kokila kujat shravan sunat sukhdai
bolat khag mriga dhenu charat trina harita bhaum man bhai
anand barsat govardhana prema punj rahyo chhai
lavanya nidhi guna nidhi anga anga prati mope barani na jaai
Krishna das gopal lal par baar baar bali jaai

"The Lord of Govardhana plays on the hill. Amidst his friends, he shines, stealing hearts of onlookers and playing his flute. The forest of vrindavana is resplendent with blossomed flowers and fruits on which bees make buzzing sounds. The peacocks and cuckoos make sounds of kuhu kuhu which delight the heart. While the birds and deers make different sounds, the calves graze on the green lands. Govardhana seems to be raining with ambrosia of love all around its vicinity. The reservoir of youthfulness and all qualities, I am not able to fully describe Gopala. Krishna das sings that he simply wards off the evil eye!"

Playing with nature and mending the calves was work enough for the time to swiftly pass away. As the sun began to shine right above the heads, the boys settled down for lunch under a shady banyan tree in the valley. Seated in a semicircle, in a very ritualistic manner, they began to open their lunch packs. Each one gasped with excitement at the wonderful dishes made by their mothers. Pure sattvik food has such a vast variety of preparations that the dishes in their lunchpacks were never repeated on consecutive days.

Special sweets for lunch

Lunch began and love spread through large wavelengths as the food was not only shared among the boys, but also given to the deers, monkeys and birds around Govardhana. As the laughed and finished their lunch, Madhu had something to say.

"Krishna! Don't you think that we had less sweets today? Also, the butter given by our mothers became slightly melted and I'm longing to have some fresh buttermilk."

"That's Madhu for you all! Never satisfied with goodies!" laughed out Gobhat.

The boys joined in too but Krishna also had something to say.

"Actually, today I fully agree with Madhu. I need more goodies too and I know exactly where to get them from. Madhu and I shall go, who will come with us?"

"Sudama and Tosha will go. We shall remain back with the calves. But don't wander away far, I have your responsibility on me. Come back soon." Balarama gave his permission.

"Where are we going Krishna?" asked Madhu trying hard to keep up with the speed after having a heavy lunch.

"Heading straight to Sakari Khor Madhu! The gopis will be passing through there any time from now. They will be carrying buttermilk, butter and milk sweets. You better cope up with us and run faster else we will miss them." replied Krishna

Sakari khor is a special pass way at Barsana, near Govardhana. Embedded by his rocks, the path allows only one person to go through at a time. The boys reached Sakari khor right in time. And Krishna immediately went and stood in the path way. The gopis approached the trail and requested Krishna to leave, but he had some other plans.

(Courtesy: brajdarshan.in)

nanda nandana daan niberatu ri
rakhahu roki dadhi samet gvalini sakha brinda prati teratu ri
jab uthhi chali prabal gopijan tab aage hvai gheratu ri
bandhi jathar pata peet lalita gati kar gahi lakuti pheratu ri
paramanand prabhu rasik siromani musaki kanakhiyan heratu ri

"Nanda nandana demands taxes! He stops the crossing of the gopikas and asks for curds, together with his friends. When the gopis try to strongly pass through, he stands up and stops them. He ties the yellow garment on his hips and holds the herding stick in his hands. The Lord of Paramanand is the crown jewel of enchanters, he gives them sidelong glances and steals their hearts."

"Krishna, please let us go through fast. Our curds and butter will get all spoilt by them time we reach home if we stand for long in the sun. We have just completed worship at the temple and are taking the offerings back home for all elders." said a gopi.

"Oh yes you may, my dear damsel! But have you not heard that the king of Vraja has announced that sakari khor is now a private pass way and no trespassers are allowed?" said Sudama standing in the trail.

"The King of vraja?! Who has made such an announcement? We have not heard of this." said one of the gopis.

"You don't know who the king of vraja is? Oh! Look, he stands here with this herding stick looking so lovingly at you – our Krishna!" Tosha was as confident as a King in his reply.

"Krishna!" the gopis laughed out.

"Oh really! Very interesting! When was the crowning ceremony held? Were we not invited? We are not witness to the kingship of your friend and reckon no announcements regarding Sakari Khor. We are getting late, please move away!" the ladies appeared slightly serious.

"Oh you handsome lad! Move on to your own path! Why do you stop the trails of the gopikas? What do you need to say? Please say it from afar, you need not touch our pots please! His pranks are becoming intolerable, there is simply no way to escape him! The gopis insist to the Lord of Govind das not to enquire about their goodies and go on and mind the huge herds of cows!"

"Look here dear ladies, if you wish to pass through this narrow path, you have to give our king taxes. There is no other way." Sudama responded in a similar tone.

"Yes you better do, because if I decide to stand in that path way, you will spend the entire day trying to push me out!" this time Madhu was proud of his chubby belly!

Everyone laughed. The gopis decided that there was no option. They need to let go off some of their goodies lest the whole stock gets spoilt while arguing with the boys.

"Okay, we shall give your king the taxes."

Krishna smiled as he accepted the curds, butter milk, butter and a few sweets from the gopis. The girls of vraja were filled with even more love, small cold tears flowed from their eyes rubbing away the kohl slightly, acknowledging the beautiful moments that they got to spend while having the association of Krishna.

The boys ran back and enjoyed the goodies telling the stories among themselves. The gopis moved on to their destinations, contented in hearts.

Before long, the sun began approaching the western horizon painting the setting sky in pretty pinks and lustrous golds. The musicians began to practice the raga poorvi which represents the eastern view of the setting sun. Govardhana's gems began to shed lights towards the western side as the sun shed its rays in that direction.

Although there were gems and ores of precious metals in the caves of Govardhana, all of it was untouched; the only reason being that it was not needed. Everyone was satisfied. And what was not needed was not disturbed unnecessarily. There was no theft and robbery; even from nature. This resulted in the land glowing with glamour of goodness.

"Collect them all. Make sure Hamsi doesn't wander into the water streams again. She never wants to get of water." said Krishna instructing his friends.

"I have her in capture together with Harini!" exclaimed Sudama holding the two calves.

"Haha! Well done! Let's get them together and move home now." said Shridama.

Krishna played his flute, the calves numbered in thousands, clustered and began to move ahead. His friends followed; some singing, some blowing horns, some collecting peacock feathers and some simply staring at Krishna!

As the sun set...

As they all approached Nandgaon, the ladies gathered together awaiting their arrival which was long hinted by the flute of Krishna, horns and singings of the boys and the bells on the calves' necks.

ban te nava rang giridhar aavat
aage re godhan paachhe aapun dhai dhai ahatavat
baruha mukut daam mani gunja benu rasal bajavat
sapta surani bar rag ragini megh gira madhu gavat
gopa sutani ke sang birajat aru kal kamal phiravat
paramanand swami ki leela sur nar muni man gavat

"The ever fresh and colourful Giridhar comes from the forest! The calves are ahead and he runs behind them. He wears a peacock feather in his crown and has the gunja flowers for his waistbelt. He plays the flute beautifully resounding the ragas that contain all the seven notes. His sound is as grave as the cloud and sweet at the same time. He comes along with his friends and holds a lotus flower in his hands. These activities of the lord of paramanand are sung of by the demigods, men and ascetics."

Two oceans of love submerged in each other as the residents of vraja and the boys met each other after the whole day. The mothers dusted off the soil from the bodies of the boys, servants assisted with the lunch packs and pharaphanelia while the elder gopas handled the cows who had met their calves after a long time too.

Each moment was a fresh one in vraja. Everyone experienced a never ending happiness at every point in time. As the day faded, they spent memorable times together and waited for the next ecstatic day to begin. The cycle repeated but was new every time.

Those seeking a fraction of this sublime happiness will still find it in the land of vraja, hidden in the shrubs, in the rocks of Govardhana, deep in the waters of Yamuna, in the voice of saints, in the experience of the devotees and in the shelter of the spiritual master.

The Never Ending Conclusion

Each day passed with so much ease in vraja. It is still as resplendent as before, irrespective of the modernity taking over at a very fast speed. One has to have the divinity in sight to view and purity in mind to experience the bliss. Vraja – a portion of the supreme abode of the supreme Lord which he passed on to mother earth, for the benefit of his loving devotees, is a land that acted as a stage for the pastimes that the Lord performed for the benefit of not only his devotees but everyone in general. For whoever sings, listens, reads or remembers these pastimes is sure to attain bliss.

Having described the leelas of the Lord, it is important to clarify that the above description is not just a layout of a legend or history that has occurred and been passed on to devotees year after year through disciplic succession. Krishna leela is an ever on-going commotion, something that is always happening. Brahma Samhita states that Krishna eternally resides in Goloka – *goloka eva nivasatyakhilatma bhooto,* and continues to perform these pastimes at every moment.

The land of vraja that we have today is part and parcel of the supreme spiritual world of Goloka that has been gifted to the devotees of this planet by the Lord on the pretext of his arrival here. The pastimes that he performed here and left are but a fraction of his vast leelas that have no end. The Vedas sing of his pastimes, his glories and his names at each moment and yet conclude with the sutra – *neti neti*. Meaning "this is not the end, this is not the end!"

Krishna performs regular activities and leelas with his nitya sidhha, nitya mukta bhaktas who have cleansed the inner self completely to relish him for eternity in the supreme world of Goloka. In those planets, the time does not pass. Every moment is lived but the strength and characteristic of time representing its ever-moving nature comes to a standstill there. Quoting again from Brahma Samhita – *nimeshardhakhyo va vrajati na hi yatrapi samaya:* - which means that even a fraction of second does not pass in the spiritual planet, and every moment is lived to the fullest. In such a realm of pure bliss, the Lord continues to perform his leelas without any break which constantly enchant the hearts of all pure souls in the universe – *leelayitena bhuvanani jayatyajastram.*

There can be no definite conclusion for the leelas of the Lord. He is omnipotent and omnipresent in his bodily form which always shines in Goloka. When he expands, he becomes the universe. The Netherlands are his feet, the sky his navel and the air are his breath. The sun and moon are his eyes, the fire element emanates from his mouth and directions are his ears. He is the universe, the very cause of all causes that is happening in the universe too. He protects and gives shelter. There is no existence without him. With such vastness, when he is loved by the purest of souls, he becomes their loved one. He becomes one of them and intermingles with them. He enjoys his true nature, emanating bliss for all receptive souls.

This description is a mere glimpse of the immense and immeasurable potencies of the supreme. But as the Ishopanishad says: *poornasya poornamadaya poornamevavashishyate* – meaning that the Lord represents the ultimate completeness and when a portion of that completeness is taken out, the portion remain complete and the complete is not distorted. Therefore, following the words of the shastras, this description is complete and has the ability to successfully drown the woe-dried hearts in the ocean of pure bliss.

This is an offering of devotion at the lotus feet of Sri Sri Radha Manvanchhit Thakur!

END NOTE

Thank you very much for reading this book! This is my third book from last year and I hope you have enjoyed reading it just as much as I did preparing it. My works are based are mostly based on ancient Indian scriptures and legends because I strongly feel that it is something of utter importance that has been left behind. There are so many solutions to general problems that can be found by simply relating to these texts and they can act as a barrier from depression, suicide and lots of negativity. I hope that this work has helped you to build a certain level of positivity within your mind! Also, if you have had a good time with this book, drop in a review! It will help other interested readers to reach the book!

If you enjoy reading similar topics, do check out some of my other books as listed below:

https://www.amazon.com/dp/B082WWSRM3

https://www.amazon.com/dp/B084CTPVLL

You may reach me at ojaswitaauthor@gmail.com. If you have any suggestions for future writings, do give a shout!